ENDLESS LIFE

Books by Lawrence Ferlinghetti

POETRY
Pictures of the Gone World
A Coney Island of the Mind
Starting from San Francisco
The Secret Meaning of Things
Back Roads to Far Places
Open Eye, Open Heart
Who Are We Now?
Northwest Ecolog
Landscapes of Living & Dying

PROSE
Her
Tyrannus Nix?
The Mexican Night

PLAYS
Unfair Arguments with Existence
Routines

TRANSLATION
Paroles by Jacques Prevert

LAWRENCE FERLINGHETTI

ENDLESS LIFE

SELECTED POEMS

A NEW DIRECTIONS BOOK

Manufactured in the United States of America.
First published clothbound in 1981 and as New Directions Paperbook 516
Published simultaneously in Canada by George J. McLeod Ltd., Toronto

The poems included in this book have been selected from the following:
Pictures of the Gone World (City Lights, 1955); *A Coney Island of the
Mind* (New Directions, 1958); *Starting from San Francisco* (ND, 1961);
The Secret Meaning of Things (ND, 1968); *Open Eye, Open Heart* (ND,
1973); *Who Are We Now?* (ND, 1976); *Northwest Ecolog* (City Lights,
1978); *Landscapes of Living & Dying* (ND, 1979). Also included are
"Modern Poetry Is Prose (But It Is Saying Plenty)" as published in
The Populist Manifestos by Grey Fox Press, 1981; "Retired Ballerinas,
Central Park West" which appeared on the Op-ed page of the *N.Y. Times*,
February 9, 1980; and "Endless Life" from *European Poems*, a work-in-
progress.

Library of Congress Cataloging in Publication Data

Ferlinghetti, Lawrence.
Endless life: selected poems
(A New Directions Book)
Includes index.
I. Title.
PS3511.E557E5   1981   811'.54   80-29127
ISBN 0-8112-0796-X
ISBN 0-8112-0797-8 (pbk.)

New Directions Books are published for James Laughlin
by New Directions Publishing Corporation
80 Eighth Avenue, New York 10011

To
Presley E. Bisland
&
Anna Lawrence Bisland

CONTENTS

I. *from* Pictures of the Gone World

AWAY ABOVE A HARBORFUL ...   3

IN HINTERTIME PRAXITELES ...   4

AND THE ARABS ASKED TERRIBLE QUESTIONS ...   5

SAROLLA'S WOMEN IN THEIR PICTURE HATS ...   7

FOR ALL I KNOW MAYBE SHE WAS HAPPIER ...   9

FORTUNE ...   10

AND SHE 'LIKE A YOUNG YEAR ...'   12

IT WAS A FACE WHICH DARKNESS COULD KILL ...   13

WITH BELLS FOR HOOVES IN SOUNDING STREETS ...   14

THAT FELLOW ON THE BOATTRAIN WHO INSISTED ...   16

HEAVEN ...   17

THE WORLD IS A BEAUTIFUL PLACE ...   18

READING YEATS I DO NOT THINK ...   21

SWEET AND VARIOUS THE WOODLARK ...   23

II. *from* A Coney Island of the Mind

IN GOYA'S GREATEST SCENES WE SEEM TO SEE ...   27

THE POET'S EYE OBSCENELY SEEING ...   29

SOMETIME DURING ETERNITY ...   31

THEY WERE PUTTING UP THE STATUE . . .   33

WHAT COULD SHE SAY TO THE
    FANTASTIC FOOLYBEAR . . .   35

IN GOLDEN GATE PARK THAT DAY . . .   36

SEE IT WAS LIKE THIS WHEN . . .   38

I HAVE NOT LAIN WITH BEAUTY ALL MY LIFE . . .   39

NOT LIKE DANTE . . .   41

CONSTANTLY RISKING ABSURDITY . . .   43

THE PENNYCANDYSTORE BEYOND THE EL . . .   45

DOVE STA AMORE . . .   46

AUTOBIOGRAPHY   47

DOG   56

I AM WAITING   59

III. *from* Starting from San Francisco

HIDDEN DOOR   65

UNDERWEAR   69

COME LIE WITH ME AND BE MY LOVE   72

THE GREAT CHINESE DRAGON   73

IV. *from* The Secret Meaning of Things

ASSASSINATION RAGA   81

MOSCOW IN THE WILDERNESS, SEGOVIA IN THE SNOW   88

V. *from* Open Eye, Open Heart

TRUE CONFESSIONAL	97
IN A TIME OF REVOLUTION FOR INSTANCE	100
STONE REALITY MEDITATION	103
SUNRISE, BOLINAS	104
A PHOENIX AT FIFTY	105
THE MAN WHO RODE AWAY	107
AN ELEGY ON THE DEATH OF KENNETH PATCHEN	110
AN IMAGINARY HAPPENING, LONDON	113
THOUGHTS TO A CONCERTO OF TELEMANN	114
TOC TOC: A COUPLE OBSERVED	116
POUND AT SPOLETO	117
ON THE TRANSSIBERIAN	119
RECIPE FOR HAPPINESS IN KHABAROVSY OR ANYPLACE	120
SALUTE	121
THIRD WORLD CALLING	123
BASEBALL CANTO	125
LAUGHING & CRYING	128
NIGHT LIGHT	130

VI. *from* Who Are We Now

DIRECTOR OF ALIENATION	133
WILD DREAMS OF A NEW BEGINNING	137

LOST PARENTS   139

PEOPLE GETTING DIVORCED   141

SHORT STORY ON A PAINTING OF GUSTAV KLIMT   142

ALIENATION: TWO BEES   144

OLBER'S PARADOX   146

UPON REFLECTION   147

DEEP CHESS   148

A MEETING OF EYES IN MEXICO   150

THE GENERAL SONG OF HUMANITY   152

EIGHT PEOPLE ON A GOLF COURSE
     AND ONE BIRD OF FREEDOM FYING OVER   154

POPULIST MANIFESTO   156

VII. *from* Northwest Ecolog

THE OLD SAILORS   163

WILD LIFE CAMEO, EARY MORN   164

READING APOLLINAIRE BY THE ROGUE RIVER   165

HORSES AT DAWN   167

INTO THE DEEPER POOLS . . .   168

ROUGH SONG OF ANIMALS DYING   170

VIII. *from* Landscapes of Living & Dying

THE OLD ITALIANS DYING   175

THE SEA AND OURSELVES AT CAPE ANN   179

A SWEET FLYING DREAM   182

TWO SCAVENGERS IN A TRUCK,
    TWO BEAUTIFUL PEOPLE IN A MERCEDES   184

THE BILLBOARD PAINTERS   186

HOME HOME HOME   189

SAN JOSE SYMPHONY RECEPTION   193

WHITE ON WHITE   194

AN ELEGY TO DISPEL GLOOM   197

ADIEU A CHARLOT   199

IX. Work-in-Progress

RETIRED BALLERINAS, CENTRAL PARK WEST   207

MODERN POETRY IS PROSE
    (BUT IT IS SAYING PLENTY)   208

ENDLESS LIFE   210

INDEX OF TITLES & FIRST LINES   219

ENDLESS LIFE

from **Pictures of the Gone World**
1955

AWAY ABOVE A HARBORFUL . . .

Away above a harborful
of caulkless houses
among the charley noble chimneypots
of a rooftop rigged with clotheslines
a woman pastes up sails
upon the wind
hanging out her morning sheets
with wooden pins
O lovely mammal
her nearly naked breasts
throw taut shadows
when she stretches up
to hang at last the last of her
so white washed sins
but it is wetly amorous
and winds itself about her
clinging to her skin
So caught with arms
uppraised
she tosses back her head
in voiceless laughter
and in choiceless gesture then
shakes out gold hair

while in the reachless seascape spaces

between the blown white shrouds

stand out the bright steamers

to kingdom come

IN HINTERTIME PRAXITELES . . .

In hintertime Praxiteles
      laid about him with a golden maul
striking into stone
        his alabaster ideals
uttering all
    the sculptor's lexicon
         in visible syllables
   He cast bronze trees
       petrified a chameleon on one
   made stone doves
      fly
     His calipers measured bridges
     and lovers
    and certain other superhumans whom
he caught upon their dusty way
        to death

   They never reached it then

       You still can almost see
     their breath
       Their stone eyes staring
thru three thousand years
      allay our fears of aging

   although Praxiteles himself
        at twenty-eight lay dead

   for sculpture isn't for
       young men
    as Constantin Brancusi
       at a later hour
    said

AND THE ARABS ASKED TERRIBLE QUESTIONS . . .

And the Arabs asked terrible questions
and the Pope didn't know what to say and the people
ran around in wooden shoes asking which way was the
head of Midas facing and everyone said

No instead of Yes

While still forever in the Luxembourg
gardens in the fountains of the Medicis were the
fat red goldfish and the fat white goldfish
and the children running around the pool
pointing and piping

Des poissons rouges!
Des poissons rouges!

but they ran off
and a leaf unhooked itself
and fell upon the pool
and lay like an eye winking
circles
and then the pool was very

still

and there was a dog
just standing there
at the edge of the pool
looking down
at the tranced fish

and not barking
            or waving its funny tail or
                    anything

      so that

         for a moment then

     in the late November dusk

silence hung like a lost idea
           and a statue turned

      its head

SAROLLA'S WOMEN IN THEIR
PICTURE HATS . . .

Sarolla's women in their picture hats
stretched upon his canvas beaches
                              beguiled the Spanish
                      Impressionists

                      And were they fraudulent pictures
of the world
            the way the light played on them
                                    creating illusions
      of love?

            I cannot help but think
                        that their 'reality'
was almost as real as
                  my memory of today

            when the last sun hung on the hills
            and I heard the day falling
            like the gulls that fell
            almost to land

      while the last picnickers lay and loved
                        in the blowing yellow broom
resisted and resisting
                  tearing themselves apart

                              again

                                    again

until the last hot hung climax
which could at last no longer be resisted
made them moan

And night's trees stood up

FOR ALL I KNOW MAYBE SHE
WAS HAPPIER . . .

For all I know maybe she was happier
                                    than anyone
that lone crone in the shawl
                            on the orangecrate train
        with the little tame bird
                            in her handkerchief
                crooning
                        to it all the time
                                    mia mascotta
        mia mascotta
                        and none of the sunday excursionists
                            with their bottles and their baskets
                            paying any
                                        attention
            and the coach
                        creaking on through cornfields
                so slowly that

                        butterflies

                        blew in and out

FORTUNE . . .

F_{ortune}

has its cookies to give out

which is a good thing

since it's been a long time since

that summer in Brooklyn
when they closed off the street
one hot day
and the

FIREMEN

turned on their hoses
and all the kids ran out in it

in the middle of the street

and there were

maybe a couple dozen of us

out there

with the water squirting up

to the

sky

and all over

us

there was maybe only six of us
                              kids altogether
          running around in our
                              barefeet and birthday
       suits
              and I remember Molly but then

       the firemen stopped squirting their hoses
              all of a sudden and went
                     back in
                     their firehouse
                     and
              started playing pinochle again
                     just as if nothing
                     had ever
                              happened
while I remember Molly
                     looked at me and

       ran in

because I guess really we were the only ones there

AND SHE 'LIKE A YOUNG YEAR . . .'

And she 'like a young year
                 walking thru the earth'
in the Bois de Boulogne that time
                   or as I remember her
     stepping out of a bathtub
            in that gold flat she had
         corner of
             Boulevard des Italiens

     Oh they say she tried everything
                before the end
took up television and crosswords
                even crocheting
    and things like that
          and came to have the air
    before the end
        (as her favorite poet described her)
of 'always carrying flowers
          toward some far
              abandoned tomb'

which doesn't surprise me now
         that I come to think of it

     The struck seed was in her

IT WAS A FACE WHICH DARKNESS COULD KILL . . .

It was a face which darkness could kill
                                    in an instant
     a face as easily hurt
                         by laughter or light

          'We *think* differently at night'
                              she told me once
     lying back languidly

                         And she would quote Cocteau

'I feel there is an angel in me' she'd say
                              'whom I am constantly
                                        shocking'

          Then she would smile and look away
                    light a cigarette for me
                                        sigh and rise
     and stretch
                    her sweet anatomy

                              let fall a stocking

WITH BELLS FOR HOOVES IN SOUNDING STREETS . . .

With bells for hooves in sounding streets

that terrible horse the unicorn

came on

and cropped a medlar from a tree
and where he dropped the seed
sprang up a virgin

oh she sprang up upon his back
and rode off tittering to a stair
where pieces of string lay scattered
everywhere

Now when she saw the string so white
so lovely and so beautiful
and looking like
Innocence itself
she got down and reached for a nice
straight piece

but it had a head
and it bit
her beautiful place

So (she said)

    this is how it all began

        Next time I'll know

      But it was too late and they buried her

THAT FELLOW ON THE BOATTRAIN
WHO INSISTED . . .

That fellow on the boattrain who insisted
          on playing blackjack
         had teeth that stuck out
       like lighthouses on a rocky coast

but
he had no eyes to see
             the dusk flash past

   horses in orchards
             noiselessly running
bunches of birds
        thrown up

    and the butterflies of yesterday
       that flittered on
         my mind

HEAVEN . . .

H eaven
was only half as far that night

at the poetry recital

listening to the burnt phrases

when I heard the poet have

a rhyming erection

then look away with a

lost look

'Every animal' he said at last

'After intercourse is sad'

But the back-row lovers
looked oblivious

and glad

THE WORLD IS A BEAUTIFUL
PLACE . . .

The world is a beautiful place
                                to be born into
if you don't mind happiness
                            not always being
                                        so very much fun
        if you don't mind a touch of hell
                                now and then
                    just when everything is fine
                                because even in heaven
                            they don't sing
                                        all the time

            The world is a beautiful place
                                        to be born into
            if you don't mind some people dying
                                        all the time
                    or maybe only starving
                                    some of the time
                    which isn't half so bad
                                    if it isn't you

Oh the world is a beautiful place
                                    to be born into
            if you don't much mind
                            a few dead minds
                    in the higher places
                                    or a bomb or two
                    now and then
                                    in your upturned faces

or such other improprieties
                          as our Name Brand society
                  is prey to
                          with its men of distinction
            and its men of extinction
                          and its priests
                  and other patrolmen

                              and its various segregations
            and congressional investigations
                              and other constipations
                  that our fool flesh
                              is heir to

Yes the world is the best place of all
                          for a lot of such things as
                  making the fun scene
                              and making the love scene
and making the sad scene
                  and singing low songs and having inspirations
            and walking around
                      looking at everything
                              and smelling flowers
            and goosing statues
                      and even thinking
                              and kissing people and
            making babies and wearing pants
                              and waving hats and
                      dancing
                  and going swimming in rivers
                      on picnics
                          in the middle of the summer
            and just generally
                      'living it up'

Yes
    but then right in the middle of it
                    comes the smiling

           mortician

READING YEATS I DO NOT THINK . . .

Reading Yeats I do not think
                              of Ireland
but of midsummer New York
                              and of myself back then
            reading that copy I found
                              on the Thirdavenue El

            the El
                  with its flyhung fans
            and its signs reading
                  SPITTING IS FORBIDDEN

            the El
                  careening thru its thirdstory world
            with its thirdstory people
                  in their thirdstory doors
            looking as if they had never heard
                              of the ground

            an old dame
                  watering her plant
            or a joker in a straw
                  putting a stickpin in his peppermint tie
and looking just like he had nowhere to go
                              but coneyisland

            or an undershirted guy
                  rocking in his rocker

21

watching the El pass by
              as if he expected it to be different
     each time

      Reading Yeats I do not think
                        of Arcady
and of its woods which Yeats thought dead
                           I think instead
     of all the gone faces
             getting off at midtown places
   with their hats and their jobs
   and of that lost book I had
           with its blue cover and its white inside
where a pencilhand had written
            HORSEMAN, PASS BY!

SWEET AND VARIOUS THE WOODLARK . . .

Sweet and various the woodlark

who sings at the unbought gate

and yet how many

                    wild beasts
          how many mad
    in the civil thickets

                    Hölderlin
                              in his stone tower
    or in that kind carpenter's house
                              at Tübingen

          or then Rimbaud
                    his 'nightmare and logic'
          a sophism of madness

    But we have our own more recent
                    who also fatally assumed
    that some direct connection
                    does exist between
          language and reality
                    word and world

          which is a laugh
                    if you ask me

    I too have drunk and seen
                    the spider

from A Coney Island of the Mind
1958

IN GOYA'S GREATEST SCENES WE SEEM TO SEE . . .

In Goya's greatest scenes we seem to see
                    the people of the world
        exactly at the moment when
            they first attained the title of
                            'suffering humanity'
        They writhe upon the page
                    in a veritable rage
                            of adversity
        Heaped up
                groaning with babies and bayonets
                            under cement skies
            in an abstract landscape of blasted trees
                bent statues bats wings and beaks
                    slippery gibbets
                cadavers and carnivorous cocks
            and all the final hollering monsters
                of the
                        'imagination of disaster'
            they are so bloody real
                    it is as if they really still existed

    And they do

            Only the landscape is changed

    They still are ranged along the roads
            plagued by legionaires
                    false windmills and demented roosters

They are the same people
                    only further from home
          on freeways fifty lanes wide
                    on a concrete continent
                         spaced with bland billboards
               illustrating imbecile illusions of happiness

          The scene shows fewer tumbrils
                         but more strung-out citizens
                              in painted cars
               and they have strange license plates
               and engines
                         that devour America

THE POET'S EYE OBSCENELY
SEEING . . .

The poet's eye obscenely seeing
sees the surface of the round world
>> with its drunk rooftops
>> and wooden oiseaux on clotheslines
>> and its clay males and females
>> with hot legs and rosebud breasts
>> in rollaway beds
and its trees full of mysteries
and its Sunday parks and speechless statues
and its America
>> with its ghost towns and empty Ellis Islands
and its surrealist landscape of
>>>> mindless prairies
>>>> supermarket suburbs
>>>> steamheated cemeteries
>>>> and protesting cathedrals
a kissproof world of plastic toiletseats tampax and taxis
>> drugged store cowboys and las vegas virgins
>> disowned indians and cinemad matrons
>> unroman senators and conscientious non-objectors

and all the other fatal shorn-up fragments

of the immigrant's dream come too true

and mislaid

among the sunbathers

SOMETIME DURING ETERNITY . . .

Sometime during eternity
                    some guys show up
and one of them
                    who shows up real late
                              is a kind of carpenter
          from some square-type place
                              like Galilee
          and he starts wailing
                    and claiming he is hip
          to who made heaven
                              and earth
                                   and that the cat
               who really laid it on us
                         is his Dad

     And moreover
          he adds
               It's all writ down
                         on some scroll-type parchments
          which some henchmen
               leave lying around the Dead Sea somewheres
               a long time ago
                         and which you won't even find
          for a coupla thousand years or so
                              or at least for
     nineteen hundred and fortyseven
                                   of them
               to be exact
                         and even then
          nobody really believes them
                              or me
                                   for that matter

You're hot
              they tell him

And they cool him

They stretch him on the Tree to cool

              And everybody after that
                            is always making models
                      of this Tree
                            with Him hung up
and always crooning His name
                      and calling Him to come down
              and sit in
                      on their combo
              as if he is *the* king cat
                            who's got to blow
       or they can't quite make it

       Only he don't come down
                            from His Tree

Him just hang there
                      on His Tree
       looking real Petered out
                      and real cool
                            and also
              according to a roundup
                            of late world news
       from the usual unreliable sources
                            real dead

THEY WERE PUTTING UP THE STATUE . . .

They were putting up the statue
    of Saint Francis
   in front of the church
    of Saint Francis
     in the city of San Francisco
 in a little side street
    just off the Avenue
        where no birds sang
  and the sun was coming up on time
        in its usual fashion
   and just beginning to shine
     on the statue of Saint Francis
  where no birds sang

And a lot of old Italians
      were standing all around
  in the little side street
     just off the Avenue
  watching the wily workers
     who were hoisting up the statue
with a chain and a crane
    and other implements
 And a lot of young reporters
     in button-down clothes
 were taking down the words
    of one young priest
 who was propping up the statue
     with all his arguments

And all the while
   while no birds sang
    any Saint Francis Passion

and while the lookers kept looking
                                    up at Saint Francis
            with his arms outstretched
                            to the birds which weren't there
        a very tall and very purely naked
                                            young virgin
            with very long and very straight
                                straw hair
            and wearing only a very small
                                        bird's nest
            in a very existential place
                                kept passing thru the crowd
                                        all the while
                and up and down the steps
                                in front of Saint Francis
            her eyes downcast all the while
                                        and singing to herself

WHAT COULD SHE SAY TO THE FANTASTIC FOOLYBEAR . . .

What could she say to the fantastic foolybear
and what could she say to brother
and what could she say
                        to the cat with future feet
and what could she say to mother
after that time that she lay lush
                        among the lolly flowers
        on that hot riverbank
                where ferns fell away in the broken air
                        of the breath of her lover
    and birds went mad
                        and threw themselves from trees
to taste still hot upon the ground
                        the spilled sperm seed

IN GOLDEN GATE PARK THAT DAY . . .

In Golden Gate Park that day
                   a man and his wife were coming along
        thru the enormous meadow
              which was the meadow of the world
He was wearing green suspenders
               and carrying an old beat-up flute
                    in one hand
    while his wife had a bunch of grapes
            which she kept handing out
                  individually
              to various squirrels
                 as if each
             were a little joke

And then the two of them came on
               thru the enormous meadow
which was the meadow of the world
            and then
     at a very still spot where the trees dreamed
   and seemed to have been waiting thru all time
                for them
    they sat down together on the grass
            without looking at each other
   and ate oranges
        without looking at each other
            and put the peels

in a basket which they seemed
                          to have brought for that purpose
            without looking at each other

And then
            he took his shirt and undershirt off
    but kept his hat on
                      sideways
                              and without saying anything
        fell asleep under it
                          And his wife just sat there looking
at the birds which flew about
    calling to each other
                in the stilly air
        as if they were questioning existence
                or trying to recall something forgotten

But then finally
                she too lay down flat
                            and just lay there looking up
                                        at nothing
            yet fingering the old flute
                                which nobody played
                and finally looking over
                                at him
        without any particular expression
                              except a certain awful look
            of terrible depression

SEE IT WAS LIKE THIS WHEN . . .

See
   it was like this when
                  we waltz into this place
a couple of Papish cats
                  is doing an Aztec two-step
And I says
            Dad let's cut
but then this dame
                  comes up behind me see
                        and says
            You and me could really exist
Wow I says
            Only the next day
            she has bad teeth
                  and really hates
                                    poetry

I HAVE NOT LAIN WITH BEAUTY
ALL MY LIFE . . .

I have not lain with beauty all my life
           telling over to myself
                          its most rife charms

    I have not lain with beauty all my life
                             and lied with it as well
               telling over to myself
                      how beauty never dies
                but lies apart
                      among the aborigines
                                    of art
                  and far above the battlefields
                                    of love

         It is above all that
                          oh yes
         It sits upon the choicest of
                          Church seats
         up there where art directors meet
    to choose the things for immortality

                          And they have lain with beauty
                    all their lives
                          And they have fed on honeydew
         and drunk the wines of Paradise
                          so that they know exactly how
               a thing of beauty is a joy
                    forever and forever
                             and how it never never
                  quite can fade
                             into a money-losing nothingness

Oh no I have not lain
                         on Beauty Rests like this
          afraid to rise at night
                   for fear that I might somehow miss
     some movement beauty might have made
          Yet I have slept with beauty
                              in my own weird way
     and I have made a hungry scene or two
                         with beauty in my bed
and so spilled out another poem or two
     and so spilled out another poem or two
                         upon the Bosch-like world

NOT LIKE DANTE . . .

Not like Dante

    discovering a *commedia*

        upon the slopes of heaven

I would paint a different kind

    of Paradiso

in which the people would be naked

    as they always are

        in scenes like that

    because it is supposed to be

    a painting of their souls

but there would be no anxious angels telling them

    how heaven is

    the perfect picture of

        a monarchy

and there would be no fires burning

        in the hellish holes below

      in which I might have stepped

nor any altars in the sky except

                  fountains of imagination

CONSTANTLY RISKING
ABSURDITY . . .

Constantly risking absurdity
                          and death
            whenever he performs
                        above the heads
                                of his audience
        the poet like an acrobat
                    climbs on rime
                        to a high wire of his own making
and balancing on eyebeams
                            above a sea of faces
            paces his way
                        to the other side of day
        performing entrechats
                        and sleight-of-foot tricks
    and other high theatrics
                        and all without mistaking
                any thing
                        for what it may not be

    For he's the super realist
                        who must perforce perceive
                taut truth
                        before the taking of each stance or step
    in his supposed advance
                            toward that still higher perch
where Beauty stands and waits
                        with gravity
        to start her death-defying leap

And he
        a little charleychaplin man
                        who may or may not catch
        her fair eternal form
                        spreadeagled in the empty air
            of existence

THE PENNYCANDYSTORE BEYOND
THE EL . . .

The pennycandystore beyond the El
is where I first
                fell in love
                            with unreality
Jellybeans glowed in the semi-gloom
of that september afternoon
A cat upon the counter moved among
                           the licorice sticks
               and tootsie rolls
          and Oh Boy Gum

Outside the leaves were falling as they died

A wind had blown away the sun

A girl ran in
Her hair was rainy
Her breasts were breathless in the little room

Outside the leaves were falling
                    and they cried
                            Too soon! too soon!

DOVE STA AMORE . . .

Dove sta amore
Where lies love
Dove sta amore
Here lies love
The ring dove love
In lyrical delight
Hear love's hillsong
Love's true willsong
Love's low plainsong
Too sweet painsong
In passages of night
Dove sta amore
Here lies love
The ring dove love
Dove sta amore
Here lies love

AUTOBIOGRAPHY

I am leading a quiet life
in Mike's Place every day
watching the champs
of the Dante Billiard Parlor
and the French pinball addicts.
I am leading a quiet life
on lower East Broadway.
I am an American.
I was an American boy.
I read the American Boy Magazine
and became a boy scout
in the suburbs.
I thought I was Tom Sawyer
catching crayfish in the Bronx River
and imagining the Mississippi.
I had a baseball mit
and an American Flyer bike.
I delivered the Woman's Home Companion
at five in the afternoon
or the Herald Trib
at five in the morning.
I still can hear the paper thump
on lost porches.
I had an unhappy childhood.
I saw Lindberg land.
I looked homeward
and saw no angel.
I got caught stealing pencils
from the Five and Ten Cent Store
the same month I made Eagle Scout.
I chopped trees for the CCC
and sat on them.

I landed in Normandy
in a rowboat that turned over.
I have seen the educated armies
on the beach at Dover.
I have seen Egyptian pilots in purple clouds
shopkeepers rolling up their blinds
at midday
potato salad and dandelions
at anarchist picnics.
I am reading 'Lorna Doone'
and a life of John Most
terror of the industrialist
a bomb on his desk at all times.
I have seen the garbagemen parade
in the Columbus Day Parade
behind the glib
farting trumpeters.
I have not been out to the Cloisters
in a long time
nor to the Tuileries
but I still keep thinking
of going.
I have seen the garbagemen parade
when it was snowing.
I have eaten hotdogs in ballparks.
I have heard the Gettysburg Address
and the Ginsberg Address.
I like it here
and I won't go back
where I came from.
I too have ridden boxcars boxcars boxcars.
I have travelled among unknown men.
I have been in Asia
with Noah in the Ark.
I was in India
when Rome was built.

I have been in the Manger
with an Ass.
I have seen the Eternal Distributor
from a White Hill
in South San Francisco
and the Laughing Woman at Loona Park
outside the Fun House
in a great rainstorm
still laughing.
I have heard the sound of revelry
by night.
I have wandered lonely
as a crowd.
I am leading a quiet life
outside of Mike's Place every day
watching the world walk by
in its curious shoes.
I once started out
to walk around the world
but ended up in Brooklyn.
That Bridge was too much for me.
I have engaged in silence
exile and cunning.
I flew too near the sun
and my wax wings fell off.
I am looking for my Old Man
whom I never knew.
I am looking for the Lost Leader
with whom I flew.
Young men should be explorers.
Home is where one starts from.
But Mother never told me
there'd be scenes like this.
Womb-weary
I rest
I have travelled.

I have seen goof city.
I have seen the mass mess.
I have heard Kid Ory cry.
I have heard a trombone preach.
I have heard Debussy
strained thru a sheet.
I have slept in a hundred islands
where books were trees.
I have heard the birds
that sound like bells.
I have worn grey flannel trousers
and walked upon the beach of hell.
I have dwelt in a hundred cities
where trees were books.
What subways what taxis what cafes!
What women with blind breasts
limbs lost among skyscrapers!
I have seen the statues of heroes
at carrefours.
Danton weeping at a metro entrance
Columbus in Barcelona
pointing Westward up the Ramblas
toward the American Express
Lincoln in his stony chair
And a great Stone Face
in North Dakota.
I know that Columbus
did not invent America.
I have heard a hundred housebroken Ezra Pounds.
They should all be freed.
It is long since I was a herdsman.
I am leading a quiet life
in Mike's Place every day
reading the Classified columns.
I have read the Reader's Digest
from cover to cover

and noted the close identification
of the United States and the Promised Land
where every coin is marked
In God We Trust
but the dollar bills do not have it
being gods unto themselves.
I read the Want Ads daily
looking for a stone a leaf
an unfound door.
I hear America singing
in the Yellow Pages.
One could never tell
the soul has its rages.
I read the papers every day
and hear humanity amiss
in the sad plethora of print.
I see where Walden Pond has been drained
to make an amusement park.
I see they're making Melville
eat his whale.
I see another war is coming
but I won't be there to fight it.
I have read the writing
on the outhouse wall.
I helped Kilroy write it.
I marched up Fifth Avenue
blowing on a bugle in a tight platoon
but hurried back to the Casbah
looking for my dog.
I see a similarity
between dogs and me.
Dogs are the true observers
walking up and down the world
thru the Molloy country.
I have walked down alleys
too narrow for Chryslers.

I have seen a hundred horseless milkwagons
in a vacant lot in Astoria.
Ben Shahn never painted them
but they're there
askew in Astoria.
I have heard the junkman's obbligato.
I have ridden superhighways
and believed the billboard's promises
Crossed the Jersey Flats
and seen the Cities of the Plain
And wallowed in the wilds of Westchester
with its roving bands of natives
in stationwagons.
I have seen them.
I am the man.
I was there.
I suffered
somewhat.
I am an American.
I have a passport.
I did not suffer in public.
And I'm too young to die.
I am a selfmade man.
And I have plans for the future.
I am in line
for a top job.
I may be moving on
to Detroit.
I am only temporarily
a tie salesman.
I am a good Joe.
I am an open book
to my boss.
I am a complete mystery
to my closest friends.

I am leading a quiet life
in Mike's Place every day
contemplating my navel.
I am a part
of the body's long madness.
I have wandered in various nightwoods.
I have leaned in drunken doorways.
I have written wild stories
without punctuation.
I am the man.
I was there.
I suffered
somewhat.
I have sat in an uneasy chair.
I am a tear of the sun.
I am a hill
where poets run.
I invented the alphabet
after watching the flight of cranes
who made letters with their legs.
I am a lake upon a plain.
I am a word
in a tree.
I am a hill of poetry.
I am a raid
on the inarticulate.
I have dreamt
that all my teeth fell out
but my tongue lived
to tell the tale.
For I am a still
of poetry.
I am a bank of song.
I am a playerpiano
in an abandoned casino

on a seaside esplanade
in a dense fog
still playing.
I see a similarity
between the Laughing Woman
and myself.
I have heard the sound of summer
in the rain.
I have seen girls on boardwalks
have complicated sensations.
I understand their hesitations.
I am a gatherer of fruit.
I have seen how kisses
cause euphoria.
I have risked enchantment.
I have seen the Virgin
in an appletree at Chartres
And Saint Joan burn
at the Bella Union.
I have seen giraffes in junglejims
their necks like love
wound around the iron circumstances
of the world.
I have seen the Venus Aphrodite
armless in her drafty corridor.
I have heard a siren sing
at One Fifth Avenue.
I have seen the White Goddess dancing
in the Rue des Beaux Arts
on the Fourteenth of July
and the Beautiful Dame Without Mercy
picking her nose in Chumley's.
She did not speak English.
She had yellow hair
and a hoarse voice
and no bird sang.

I am leading a quiet life
in Mike's Place every day
watching the pocket pool players
making the minestrone scene
wolfing the macaronis
and I have read somewhere
the Meaning of Existence
yet have forgotten
just exactly where.
But I am the man
And I'll be there.
And I may cause the lips
of those who are asleep
to speak.
And I may make my notebooks
into sheaves of grass.
And I may write my own
eponymous epitaph
instructing the horsemen
to pass.

DOG

The dog trots freely in the street
and sees reality
and the things he sees
are bigger than himself
and the things he sees
are his reality
Drunks in doorways
Moons on trees
The dog trots freely thru the street
and the things he sees
are smaller than himself
Fish on newsprint
Ants in holes
Chickens in Chinatown windows
their heads a block away
The dog trots freely in the street
and the things he smells
smell something like himself
The dog trots freely in the street
past puddles and babies
cats and cigars
poolrooms and policemen
He doesn't hate cops
He merely has no use for them
and he goes past them
and past the dead cows hung up whole
in front of the San Francisco Meat Market
He would rather eat a tender cow
than a tough policeman
though either might do
And he goes past the Romeo Ravioli Factory
and past Coit's Tower
and past Congressman Doyle of the Unamerican Committee

56

He's afraid of Coit's Tower
but he's not afraid of Congressman Doyle
although what he hears is very discouraging
very depressing
very absurd
to a sad young dog like himself
to a serious dog like himself
But he has his own free world to live in
His own fleas to eat
He will not be muzzled
Congressman Doyle is just another
fire hydrant
to him
The dog trots freely in the street
and has his own dog's life to live
and to think about
and to reflect upon
touching and tasting and testing everything
investigating everything
without benefit of perjury
a real realist
with a real tale to tell
and a real tail to tell it with
a real live
            barking
                    democratic dog
engaged in real
                free enterprise
with something to say
                    about ontology
something to say
            about reality
                    and how to see it
                            and how to hear it
with his head cocked sideways
                    at streetcorners

as if he is just about to have
                        his picture taken
                                    for Victor Records
                    listening for
                                His Master's Voice
            and looking
                        like a living questionmark
                                    into the
                                    great gramophone
                                    of puzzling existence
            with its wondrous hollow horn
                which always seems
                just about to spout forth
                                    some Victorious answer
                                    to everything

I AM WAITING

I am waiting for my case to come up
and I am waiting
for a rebirth of wonder
and I am waiting for someone
to really discover America
and wail
and I am waiting
for the discovery
of a new symbolic western frontier
and I am waiting
for the American Eagle
to really spread its wings
and straighten up and fly right
and I am waiting
for the Age of Anxiety
to drop dead
and I am waiting
for the war to be fought
which will make the world safe
for anarchy
and I am waiting
for the final withering away
of all governments
and I am perpetually awaiting
a rebirth of wonder

I am waiting for the Second Coming
and I am waiting
for a religious revival
to sweep thru the state of Arizona
and I am waiting

for the Grapes of Wrath to be stored
and I am waiting
for them to prove
that God is really American
and I am waiting
to see God on television
piped onto church altars
if only they can find
the right channel
to tune in on
and I am waiting
for the Last Supper to be served again
with a strange new appetizer
and I am perpetually awaiting
a rebirth of wonder

I am waiting for my number to be called
and I am waiting
for the Salvation Army to take over
and I am waiting
for the meek to be blessed
and inherit the earth
without taxes
and I am waiting
for forests and animals
to reclaim the earth as theirs
and I am waiting
for a way to be devised
to destroy all nationalisms
without killing anybody
and I am waiting
for linnets and planets to fall like rain
and I am waiting for lovers and weepers
to lie down together again
in a new rebirth of wonder

I am waiting for the Great Divide to be crossed
and I am anxiously waiting
for the secret of eternal life to be discovered
by an obscure general practitioner
and I am waiting
for the storms of life
to be over
and I am waiting
to set sail for happiness
and I am waiting
for a reconstructed Mayflower
to reach America
with its picture story and tv rights
sold in advance to the natives
and I am waiting
for the lost music to sound again
in the Lost Continent
in a new rebirth of wonder

I am waiting for the day
that maketh all things clear
and I am awaiting retribution
for what America did
to Tom Sawyer
and I am waiting
for the American Boy
to take off Beauty's clothes
and get on top of her
and I am waiting
for Alice in Wonderland
to retransmit to me
her total dream of innocence
and I am waiting
for Childe Roland to come
to the final darkest tower

and I am waiting
for Aphrodite
to grow live arms
at a final disarmament conference
in a new rebirth of wonder

I am waiting
to get some intimations
of immortality
by recollecting my early childhood
and I am waiting
for the green mornings to come again
youth's dumb green fields come back again
and I am waiting
for some strains of unpremeditated art
to shake my typewriter
and I am waiting to write
the great indelible poem
and I am waiting
for the last long careless rapture
and I am perpetually waiting
for the fleeing lovers on the Grecian Urn
to catch each other up at last
and embrace
and I am awaiting
perpetually and forever
a renaissance of wonder

from Starting from San Francisco
1961

HIDDEN DOOR
(*Hymn to Machu Picchu, after Neruda*)

Hidden door dead secret
          which is Mother
Hidden door dead secret
          which is Father
Hidden door dead secret
          of our buried life
Hidden door behind which man carries
          his footprints along the streets
Hidden door of clay hands knocking
Hidden door without handles
          whose life is made of knocks
          by hand and foot
          Poor hand poor foot poor life!
Hidden door with hair for hinges
Hidden door with lips for latches
Hidden door with skeletons for keys
Hidden door autobiography of humanity
Hidden door dictionary of the universe
Hidden door palimpsest of myself
Hidden door I'm made of
          with my sticks of limbs
Hidden door pathetic fallacy
          of the evidence of the senses
          as to the nature of reality
Hidden door in blind eyes of termites
          that knock knock
Hidden door blind man with tin cup
          on a stone corner deaf and dumb
Hidden door train-whistle lost
          in book of night
Hidden door on night's wheels I blundering follow
          like a rhinoceros drinking through cities

Hidden door of carrier-pigeons' wings
          which have half-forgotten
          their destination
Hidden door plane's wing that skids in space
          casting stone shadow
          on sundial of earth
Hidden door flying boxcar of history
Hidden door of Sunday without church
Hidden door of animal faces animal laughter animal dreams
          and hidden door Cro-Magnon Man
          among machines
Hidden door dark forest of America
          knock knock in North Dakota
Hidden door that wings over America
          and slants over San Francisco
          and slams into the Pacific
          drifting eternally southward
          to Tierra del Fuego
          with a knock knock undersea
          at lost door of Lota coal mines
Hidden door surfboard to lost shore of light
          and hidden door floated up on tides
          like a shipwrecked coffinlid
          bearing blind mouths blind breasts blind thought
          through the centuries
Hidden door sea-angel cast-up Albatross
          spouting seasperm of love in thirty languages
          and the love-ship of life
          sunk by the poison-squid of hate
Hidden door double-winged sticky-bird plumed serpent
          stuck to moon afire forever drunk in time
          flapping loose in eternity
Hidden door of the future mystic life
          among Magellan's nebulae
          and hidden door of my mislaid
          visionary self

Hidden door San Luis rope-bridge which is man
                    hung between nature and spirit
Hidden door of the spirit seen as a fleshy thing
                    and hidden door of eyes and vulvas
                    that still open only with a key
                    of cartilage and flesh
                    and hidden door frozen Inca mummy
                    Prince of the Plomo
                    fucked to death in sun-god sacrifice
Hidden door tin cup of blind brother mutes
                    crouched on a Cuzco corner
                    blowing bamboo flutes
                    at coca midnight
Hidden door of the Andes at ten thousand feet
                    in a ragged mist of ruins and red horizons
                    with seacoast hung below
                    still lost among conquistadors
                    horses dogs and incomprehensible laws
Hidden door wild river of the Urubamba
                    upon which still floats somewhere
                    the lost herb that separates soul from body
                    and hidden door which is itself that herb
                    and hidden door which is that separation
                    and hidden door made of mirrors
                    on the waters of this river
                    in which I cannot see beyond myself
                    because my body's in the way
Hidden door at last I see through
                    beyond dear body bag of bones
                    which I leave naked on a rock
Hidden door I wigless climb to
                    beyond that river
Hidden door at last I fall through
                    in the lost end of day
It is dusk
by the time we get to

67

Machu Picchu
Some Indians go by dancing
playing their flutes
and beating drums

Peru-Chile, January-February, 1960

UNDERWEAR

I didn't get much sleep last night
thinking about underwear
Have you ever stopped to consider
underwear in the abstract
When you really dig into it
some shocking problems are raised
Underwear is something
we all have to deal with
Everyone wears
some kind of underwear
Even Indians
wear underwear
Even Cubans
wear underwear
The Pope wears underwear I hope
The Governor of Louisiana
wears underwear
I saw him on TV
He must have had tight underwear
He squirmed a lot
Underwear can really get you in a bind
You have seen the underwear ads
for men and women
so alike but so different
Women's underwear holds things up
Men's underwear holds things down
Underwear is one thing
men and women have in common
Underwear is all we have between us
You have seen the three-color pictures
with crotches encircled
to show the areas of extra strength

and three-way stretch
promising full freedom of action
Don't be deceived
It's all based on the two-party system
which doesn't allow much freedom of choice
the way things are set up
America in its Underwear
struggles thru the night
Underwear controls everything in the end
Take foundation garments for instance
They are really fascist forms
of underground government
making people believe
something but the truth
telling you what you can or can't do
Did you ever try to get around a girdle
Perhaps Non-Violent Action
is the only answer
Did Gandhi wear a girdle?
Did Lady Macbeth wear a girdle?
Was that why Macbeth murdered sleep?
And that spot she was always rubbing—
Was it really in her underwear?
Modern anglosaxon ladies
must have huge guilt complexes
always washing and washing and washing
Out damned spot
Underwear with spots very suspicious
Underwear with bulges very shocking
Underwear on clothesline a great flag of freedom
Someone has escaped his Underwear
May be naked somewhere
Help!
But don't worry
Everybody's still hung up in it

There won't be no real revolution
And poetry still the underwear of the soul
And underwear still covering
a multitude of faults
in the geological sense—
strange sedimentary stones, inscrutable cracks!
If I were you I'd keep aside
an oversize pair of winter underwear
Do not go naked into that good night
And in the meantime
keep calm and warm and dry
No use stirring ourselves up prematurely
'over Nothing'
Move forward with dignity
hand in vest
Don't get emotional
And death shall have no dominion
There's plenty of time my darling
Are we not still young and easy
Don't shout

COME LIE WITH ME AND
BE MY LOVE

Come lie with me and be my love

Love lie with me

Lie down with me

Under the cypress tree

In the sweet grasses

Where the wind lieth

Where the wind dieth

As night passes

Come lie with me

All night with me

And have enough of kissing me

And have enough of making love

And let our two selves speak

All night under the cypress tree

Without making love

THE GREAT CHINESE DRAGON

The great Chinese dragon which is the greatest dragon in all
the world and which once upon a time
was towed across the Pacific by a crew
of coolies rowing in an open boat—was
the first real live dragon ever actually
to reach these shores
And the great Chinese dragon passing thru the Golden Gate
sprouting streams of water like a string
of fireboats then broke loose somewhere
near China Camp gulped down a hun-
dred Chinese seamen and forthwith ate
up all the shrimp in San Francisco Bay
And the great Chinese dragon was therefore forever after
confined in a Chinatown basement and
ever since allowed out only for Chinese
New Year's parades and other Un-
american demonstrations paternally
watched-over by those benevolent men
in blue who represent our more ad-
vanced civilization which has reached
such a high state of democracy as to
allow even a few barbarians to carry on
their quaint native customs in our
midst
And thus the great Chinese dragon which is the greatest
dragon in all the world now can only
be seen creeping out of an Adler Alley
cellar like a worm out of a hole some-
time during the second week in Feb-
ruary every year when it sorties out of
hibernation in its Chinese storeroom
pushed from behind by a band of forty-

73

three Chinese electricians and technicians who stuff its peristaltic accordion-body up thru a sidewalk delivery entrance

And first the swaying snout appears and then the eyes at ground level feeling along the curb and then the head itself casting about and swaying and heaving finally up to the corner of Grant Avenue itself where a huge paper sign proclaims the *World's Largest Chinatown*

And the great Chinese dragon's jaws wired permanently agape as if by a demented dentist to display the Cadmium teeth as the hungry head heaves out into Grant Avenue right under the sign and raising itself with a great snort of fire suddenly proclaims the official firecracker start of the Chinese New Year

And the lightbulb eyes lighting up and popping out on coiled wire springs and the body stretching and rocking further and further around the corner and down Grant Avenue like a caterpillar roller coaster with the eyes sprung out and waving in the air like the blind feelers of some mechanical preying mantis and the eyes blinking on and off with Chinese red pupils and tiny bamboo-blind eyelids going up and down

And still the tail of the dragon in the Adler Alley cellar uncoiling and unwinding out into the street with the fortythree Chinese technicians still stuffing the dragon out the hole in the sidewalk and the head of the dragon now three blocks away in

the middle of the parade of fancy floats
presided over by Chinese virgins
And here comes the St. Mary's Chinese Girls' Drum Corps
and here come sixteen white men in
pith helmets beating big bass drums
representing the Order of the Moose
and here comes a gang of happy car
salesmen disguised as Islam Shriners
and here comes a chapter of the Order
of Improved Red Men and here comes
a cordon of motorcycle cops in crash
helmets with radios going followed by
a small papier-mâché lion fed with
Necco wafers and run by two guys left
over from a Ten-Ten festival which in
turn is followed by the great Chinese
dragon itself gooking over balconies as
it comes
And the great Chinese dragon has eaten a hundred humans
and their legs pop out of his underside
and are his walking legs which are not
mentioned in the official printed pro-
gram in which he is written up as the
Great Golden Dragon made in Hong
Kong to the specifications of the Chi-
nese Chamber of Commerce and he
represents the force and mystery of life
and his head sways in the sky between
the balconies as he comes followed by
six Chinese boy scouts wearing Keds
and carrying strings of batteries that
light up the dragon like a nighttime
freeway
And he has lain all winter among a heap of collapsed paper
lanterns and green rubber lizards and
ivory backscratchers with the iron side-

walk doors closed over his head but he
has now sprung up with the first sign
of Spring like the force of life itself
and his head sways in the sky and
gooks in green windows as he comes
And he is a monster with the head of a dog and the body
of a serpent risen yearly out of the sea
to devour a virgin thrown from a cliff
to appease him and he is a young man
handsome and drunk ogling the girls
and he has high ideals and a hundred
sport shoes and he says No to Mother
and he is a big red table the world will
never tilt and he has big eyes every-
where thru which he sees all woman-
kind milkwhite and dove-breasted and
he will eat their waterflowers for he is
the cat with future feet wearing Keds
and he eats cake out of pastry windows
and is hungrier and more potent and
more powerful and more omniverous
than the papier-mâché lion run by two
guys and he is the great earthworm
of lucky life filled with flowing Chinese
semen and he considers his own and
our existence in its most profound
sense as he comes and he has no Chris-
tian answer to the existential question
even as he sees the spiritual everywhere
translucent in the material world and
he does not want to escape the responsi-
bility of being a dragon or the conse-
quences of his long horny tail still
buried in the basement but the blue
citizens on their talking cycles think
that he wants to escape and at all costs

he must not be allowed to escape because the great Chinese dragon is the greatest potential dragon in all the world and if allowed to escape from Chinatown might gallop away up their new freeway at the Broadway entrance mistaking it for a Great Wall of China or some other barbarian barrier and so go careening along it chewing up stanchions and signposts and belching forth some strange disintegrating medium which might melt down the great concrete walls of America and they are afraid of how far the great Chinese dragon might really go starting from San Francisco and so they have secretly and securely tied down the very end of his tail in its hole

so that

this great pulsing phallus of life at the very end of its parade at the very end of Chinatown gives one wild orgasm of a shudder and rolls over fainting in the bright night street since even for a dragon every orgasm is a little death

And then the great Chinese dragon starts silently shrinking and shriveling up and drawing back and back and back to its first cave and the soft silk skin wrinkles up and shrinks and shrinks on its sprung bamboo bones and the handsome dejected head hangs down like a defeated prizefighter's and so is stuffed down again at last into its private place and the cellar sidewalk doors press down again over

the great wilted head with one small
hole of an eye blinking still thru the
gratings of the metal doors as the great
Chinese dragon gives one last con-
vulsive earthquake shake and rolls
over dead-dog to wait another white
year for the final coming and the final
sowing of his oats and teeth

from The Secret Meaning of Things
1968

ASSASSINATION RAGA

Tune in to a raga
on the stereo
and turn on Death TV
without its sound
Outside the plums are growing in a tree
'The force that through the green fuse
drives the flower'
drives Death TV
'A grief ago'
They lower the body soundlessly
into a huge plane in Dallas
into a huge plane in Los Angeles
marked 'United States of America'
and soundlessly
the 'United States of America'
takes off
& wings away with that Body
Tune out the TV sound
& listen soundlessly
to the blind mouths of its motors
& a sitar speaking on the stereo
a raga in a rage
at all that black death

and all that bad karma

La illaha el lill Allah

There is no god but God

The force that through the red fuze

drives the bullet

drives the needle in its dharma groove

and man the needle

drives that plane

of the 'United States of America'

through its sky full of shit & death

and the sky never ends

as it wings soundlessly

from those fucked-up cities

whose names we'd rather not remember

Inside the plane

inside the plane a wife

lies soundlessly

against the coffin

Engine whines as sitar sings outrageously

La illaha el lill Allah

There is no god but God?

There is no god but Death?

The plums are falling through the tree

The force that drives the bullet

through the gun

drives everyone

as the 'United States of America'

flies on sightlessly

through the swift fierce years

with the dead weight of its Body

which they keep flying from Dallas

which they keep flying from Los Angeles

And the plane lands

without folding its wings

its shadow in mourning for itself

withdraws into itself

in death's draggy dominion

La illaha el lill Allah

There is no god but Death?

The force that through the green fuze

drove his life

drives everyone

La illaha el lill Allah

And they are driving the Body

they are driving the Body

up Fifth Avenue

past a million people in line

'We are going to be here a long time'

says Death TV's spielman

The cortège passes soundlessly

'Goodbye! Goodbye!' some people cry
The traffic flows around & on
The force that drives the cars
combusts our karma
La illaha el lill Allah
There is no god but Death?
The force that drives our life to death
drives sitar too
so soundlessly
La illaha el lill Allah
And they lift the Body
They lift the Body
of the United States of America
and carry it into a cathedral
singing Hallelujah He Shall Live
For ever & ever
And then the Body moves again
down Fifth Avenue
Fifty-seven black sedans after it
There are people with roses
behind the barricades
in bargain-basement dresses
And sitar sings & sings nonviolence
sitar sounds in us its images of ecstasy
its depth of ecstasy

84

against old dung & death

La illaha el lill Allah

La illaha el lill Allah

The force that strikes its strings

strikes us

And the funeral train

the silver train

starts up soundlessly

at a dead speed

over the hot land

an armed helicopter over it

They are clearing the tracks ahead of assassins

The tracks are lined with bare faces

A highschool band in New Brunswick plays

The Battle Hymn of the Republic

They have shot it down again

They have shot him down again

& will shoot him down again

& take him on a train

& lower him again

into a grave in Washington

La illaha el lill Allah

Day & night journeys the coffin

through the dark land

too dark now to see the dark faces

La illaha el lill Allah

Plums & planes are falling through the air

La illaha el lill Allah

as sitar sings the only answer

sitar sings its only answer

sitar sounds the only sound

that still can still all violence

La illaha el lill Allah

There is no god but Life

Sitar says it Sitar sounds it

Sitar sounds on us to love love & hate hate

Sitar breathes its Atman breath in us

sounds & sounds in us its lovely *om om*

La illaha el lill Allah

At every step the pure wind rises

La illaha el lill Allah

People with roses

behind the barricades!

First read, to a loud evening raga, at "The Incredible Poetry Reading," Nourse Auditorium, San Francisco, June 8, 1968, the day Robert Kennedy was buried.

"Death TV": the phrase comes from "So Who Owns Death TV" by William Burroughs, Claude Pélieu & Carl Weissner.

"The force that through the green fuse drives the flower" &
"A grief ago": from Dylan Thomas. "La illaha el lill Allah":
variation of a Sufi ecstatic chant. A corruption of the Koran.
"The swift fierce years": from a phrase in Eldridge Cleaver's
"Soul On Ice."

Atman: breath, soul, life principle.
Om: originally a syllable denoting assent—the "ideal, inaudible sound" of the universe. . . .

MOSCOW IN THE WILDERNESS, SEGOVIA IN THE SNOW

Midnight Moscow Airport
   sucks me in from Siberia
 And blows me out alone
     in a black bus
    down dark straight night roads
    stark snow plains
     eternal taiga
      into monster Moscow
   stands of white birches
    ghosted in the gloaming
Where of a sudden
   Segovia bursts thru
     over the airwaves
They've let him in
     to drive the dark bus
Segovia's hands
     grasp the steering wheel
Yokels in housing projects
  drop their balalaikas & birch banjos
Segovia comes on
   like the pulse of life itself
Segovia comes on thru the snowdrifts
     and plains of La Mancha
  fields & fields & fields
    of frozen music
   melted on bus radios
Segovia at the instrument
   driving thru the night land
 of Antiquera
    Granada
     Seville

Tracery of the Alhambra
in a billion white birches
born in the snow
trills of blackbirds in them
Segovia warms his hands
                and melts Moscow
        moves his hand
                with a circular motion
                over an ivory bridge
                to gutted Stalingrads
Segovia knows no answer
He's no Goya & he's no Picasso
but also
        he's no Sleeping Gypsy With Guitar
        Guarded by a Lion
and who knows if he slept
                with Franco
He knows black condors fly
He knows a free world when he hears one
His strums are runs upon it
He does not fret
He plucks his guts
and listens to himself as he plays
and speaks to himself
and echoes himself
And he keeps driving & driving
                his instrument
        down the wide dark ways
                into great Moscow
        down the black boulevards
                past Kremlin lit & locked
                in its hard dream
                in the great Russian night
        past Bolshoi Ballet & Gorky Institute
        John Reed at the Drama Theatre
        Stalyagi & heroin at Taganka

Stone Mayakovsky stares
             thru a blizzard of white notes
                   in Russian winter light
Segovia hears his stoned cry
    and he hears the pulse in the blood
        as he listens to life as he plays
    and he keeps coming & coming
                  thru the Russian winter night
He's in Moscow but doesn't know it
He played somewhere else
                 and it comes out here
    in a thaw on an airwave
                 over Gogol's Dark People
        stark figures
           in the white night streets
      clotted in the snow
He listens to them as he goes along
He listens for a free song
              such as he hardly hears
                  back home
           Is Lenin listening
                 after fifty Octobers
Segovia walks thru the snow
             listening as he goes
         down Vorovsky Street
                 to the Writers' Union
He meets the old hairs that run it
    They dig him
            & they know what it means to dig
                in mahogany cities
Segovia teaches them open-tuning
    with which they can play anything
        freely & simply
    This is not his Master Class

He leaves them humming & goes on
Segovia plays in the loose snow
    and digs a bit alone
        under the free surface
          with his free hand
He strikes softly as he listens
He hears a dull thud
    where something is buried
      a familiar thud
    such as he sometimes hears
        back home
He turns away & goes on
        down Vorovsky Street
His music has a longing sound
He yearns & yet does not yearn
He exists & is tranquil
        in spite of all
He has no message
He is his own message
        his own ideal sound
And he sounds so lonely to himself
    as he goes on playing
      in the iron-white streets
And he is saying: I say all I know
    & I know no meaning
He is saying
      This is the song of evening
      when the sphinx lies down
      This is the song of the day
      that begins & begins
      The night lifts
        its white night-stick
      The ash of life
        dries my song

              If you only knew
He is saying
        My love my love
                  where are you
        Under the pomegranate tree
He is saying
        Where is joy where is ecstasy
        stretched out in the snow
        where only the birds are at home
He is saying
        There's a huge emptiness here
        that stares from all the faces
        All that is lost must be
                  looked for once more
He is saying
        Far from me far from me
        you are the hour & the generation
        they marked for result
He is saying
        I am your ruin
              unique & immortal
        I am your happiness unknown
        I am light
              where you are dark
              where you are heavy
He is saying
              I am an old man
              and life flowers
                  in the windows of the sun
        But where is the sun the sun
                  Soleares . . .
On the steps of a jail
        that looks like a church
              he finds a white bird

What is important in life? says the bird
Segovia says Nada but keeps on playing
        his Answer
And he cries out now
        when he sees a strange woman
            or sees a strange thing
        And he hears many strange women
            & many strange things
            after fifty Octobers
            & fifty strange springs
And Segovia follows them
            down their streets
            and into their houses
            and into their rooms
            and into the night of their beds
        And waits for them to make love
        And waits for them to speak
        And waits & waits for them to speak
And he cries out now
    when he hears them speak
        at last in their last retreat
No he doesn't cry out
He never cries out
He is taciturn & never sings
Only his instrument speaks & sings
But when it does sing
when it does cry out
at what it hears
            an ancient armadillo
    asleep for centuries
            in the cellar of the Kremlin
    raises its horny head
        opens its square third eye
    and looks around blinking

and then at last
unglues its great gut mouth
and utters
ecstatic static

Moscow-San Francisco, March, 1967

Dedicated to Andrei Voznesènsky & Yevgeni Yevtushenko

from Open Eye, Open Heart
1973

TRUE CONFESSIONAL

I was conceived in the summer of Nineteen Eighteen
(or was it Thirty Eight)
when some kind of war was going on
but it didn't stop two people
from making love in Ossining that year
I like to think on a riverbank in sun
on a picnic by the Hudson
as in a painting of the Hudson River School
or up at Bear Mountain maybe
after taking the old Hudson River Line
paddlewheel excursion steamer
(I may have added the paddlewheel—
the Hudson my Mississippi)
And on the way back she
already carried me
inside of her
I lawrence ferlinghetti
wrought from the dark in my mother long ago
born in a small back bedroom—
In the next room my brother heard
the first cry,
many years later wrote me—
"Poor Mom—No husband—No money—Pop dead—
How she went through it all—"
Someone squeezed my heart
to make it go
I cried and sprang up
Open eye open heart where
do I wander
I cried and ran off
into the heart of the world
Carried away

by another I knew not
And which of me shall know my brother?
'I am my son, my mother, my father,
I am born of myself
my own flesh sucked'
And someone squeezed my heart
to make me go
And I began to go
through my number
I was a wind-up toy
someone had dropped wound-up
into a world already
running down
The world had been going on
a long time already
but it made no difference
It was new it was like new
i made it new
i saw it shining
and it shone in the sun
and it spun in the sun
and the skein it spun
was pure light
My life was made of it
made of the skeins of light
The cobwebs of Night
were not on it
were not of it
It was too bright
to see
too luminous
to cast a shadow
and there was another world
behind the bright screens
I had only to close my eyes

for another world to appear
too near and too dear
to be anything but myself
my inside self
where everything real
was to happen
in this place which still exists
inside myself
and hasn't changed that much
certainly not as much
as the outside
with its bag of skin
and its 'aluminum beard'
and its blue blue eyes
which see as one eye
in the middle of the head
where everything happens
except what happens
in the heart
vajra lotus diamond heart
wherein I read
the poem that never ends

IN A TIME OF REVOLUTION
FOR INSTANCE

I had just ordered a fishplate at the counter when
three very beautiful
fucked-up people entered
I don't know how or why I
thought they must be
fucked-up except
they were very beautiful
two men and one very
beautiful goldenhaired
young woman very
well groomed and
wearing sports clothes like
as if they must have
just gotten out of an
old-fashioned Stutz
roadster with top
down and tennis rackets and
the woman strode to the back
of the restaurant
found a vacant table and
strode back and
got the other two
beckoning with elegant
gestures and
smiling slightly at them and
the three of them
walked back slowly to the table
as if they were not afraid
of anything or anyone
in that place and
took possession of it with

lovely expressions and
the very lovely young lady
settled herself so easily
on the settee beside
the younger of the two men
both of whom had
lightbrown wavy hair not too long
and cut like Hollywood
tennis stars or anyway
like visitors from some other town more
elegant than our own and
they were obviously so much better
looking and so much better
brought up than anyone else
in the place
they looked like they might be
related to the Kennedys and
they obviously had no Indian or Eyetalian
blood in them
and she obviously with
so many avenues open to her
with her two men
one of whom could have been
her brother
I could not imagine her *carrying*
a carbine and
she kept tossing her hair ever so gently out
of her eyes and
smiling at both of them and
at nothing in particular that I
could imagine and
her lips were moving gently with
her gentle smile and
I kept trying to imagine what
she could possibly be saying with

those perfect lips over
those perfect teeth so white
with her eyes now and then sliding
over and down the counter where
a lot of little people sat
quietly eating their quite ordinary
lunches while
the three beautiful people who
could have been anywhere
seemed just about to order
something special and
eat it with ice cream and cigarettes and
my fish finally arrived looking
not quite unfrozen and
quite plastic but
I decided to eat it anyway
she was a beautiful creature and I
felt like Charlie Chaplin eating his shoe
when her eyes slid over me
the Modern Jass Quartet
came over the Muzak speakers and
under other circumstances
in a time of revolution for instance
we might have made it

STONE REALITY MEDITATION

Humankind can indeed bear
very much reality
That 'busy little monster
                    manunkind'
can bear it too
So may womankind
So can every kind
of clay and creature
Trees too can bear it
after the leaves have flown away
after the birds have blown away
'bare ruined choirs' bear it
as stones do
They too bear the 'heavy weight
of creation'
as we do
cast in clay and stoned in earth
Masters of ecstasy

SUNRISE, BOLINAS

This little heart that remembers
                    every little thing
          begins the day
                    most of the time
                         by an attempt at singing
                              some sunny rhyme

Such effrontery, such audacity
                    in the face of everything!
Still I'll sing at the sun
                    for a beginning—

Such presumption, such perversity
                         to mistake bird-cries for song
                         when they may really be
                              cries of despair!
     As if our life
          as if all life
               were not a tragedy
                    though all is passing fair

     As if our life
               were not so very various
                    as to turn it all to litany—

O drunk flute
          O Golden Mouth
                    sing a mad song
                         to save us

A PHOENIX AT FIFTY

At new age fifty
turn inward on old self
and rock on my back in a torn green hammock
deep in a ruined garden
where first the sweet birds sang
behind a white wood cottage
at Montecito Santa Barbara
sunk in sea-vine succulents
under huge old eucalyptrees
wind blows white sunlight thru
A mute ruined statue of a nymph dancing
turns in sun
as if to sing 'When day is done'
It is not
A helicopter flies
out of an angle of the sun
its windmill choppers waving
thru the waving treetops
thru which the hot wind blows & blows
pure desire made of light
I float on my back in the sea of it
and gaze straight up into eye-white sky
as into eyes of one beloved whispering
   'Let

     me

       in'
Too bright
   too bright!
I close my eyes
lest sun thru such lenses
set me afire

but the blown light batters thru
lids and lashes
I burn and leave
no ashes

Yet will arise

THE MAN WHO RODE AWAY

(To D. H. Lawrence)

Above Taos now
                    I peer through the crack
        of your locked door
                    Dead Lawrence
and there indeed I see
                    they've got you now at last
        safely stashed away
                    locked away from the light
        of your dear sun
                    in the weird great dark
            of your little
                    shuttered shrine
with the dark brown cover
                    of your old portable
clenched like a jaw upon
                    dumb keys
                            teeth sans tongue
                as in a mute mask
                    of a Greek megaphone

        Ah here's real proof
                    the soul has its rages—
                dampered!
                    in darkness!
        shrine locked—
                    booby-trapped for burglars—
plumed serpent stoned
                    into a gargoyle!

Lawrence Lawrence bearded David
                              Phoenix flamed
             out of a mine-head
                              ash to ash
             Sown in Vence
                         and resown in America
             (del Norte)
                         Where now
                here now
                            your portable seed
             has blown away
                            Other seeds
             are growing
                         Not yours
             Lawrence
                         in the white sands
                                        proving grounds!

Lawrence now I see you come alone
from your cribbed cabin
all fenced in the backyard compound
of that big caretaker's house

You stand still a moment in the still air.

Your eyes have a Mexican look
turned South
over the arroyos
ahora y siempre

Winter is coming

You have your ticket

108

You have your blue denim jacket

You have your crazy Stetson

Your tin phoenix tacked to a tree
drops in a giftshop window

A mistral wind
rattles the pine needles
of your bones

AN ELEGY ON THE DEATH
OF KENNETH PATCHEN

A poet is born
A poet dies
And all that lies between
is us
and the world

And the world lies about it
making as if it had got his message
even though it is poetry
but most of the world wishing
it could just forget about him
and his awful strange prophecies

Along with all the other strange things
he said about the world
which were all too true
and which made them fear him
more than they loved him
though he spoke much of love
Along with all the alarms he sounded
which turned out to be false
if only for the moment
all of which made them fear his tongue
more than they loved him
Though he spoke much of love
and never lived by 'silence exile & cunning'
and was a loud conscientious objector to
the deaths we daily give each other
though we speak much of love

And when such a one dies
   even the agents of Death should take note
    and shake the shit from their wings
                      in Air Force One
  But they do not
          And the shit still flies
And the poet now is disconnected
              and won't call back
  though he spoke much of love

And still we hear him say
      'Do I not deal with angels
       when her lips I touch'
And still we hear him say
      'O my darling troubles heaven
       with her loveliness'
And still we love to hear him say
  'As we are so wonderfully done with each other
  We can walk into our separate sleep
  On floors of music where the milkwhite cloak
      of childhood lies'
And still we hear him saying
    'Therefore the constant powers do not lessen.
    Nor is the property of the spirit scattered
    on the cold hills of these events'
And still we hear him asking
    'Do the dead know what time it is?'

He is gone under
        He is scattered
              undersea
  and knows what time
     but won't be back to tell it
He would be too proud to call back anyway
  And too full of strange laughter
       to speak to us anymore anyway

111

And the weight of human experience
                    lies upon the world
        like the chains of the sea
                            in which he sings
And he swings in the tides of the sea
        And his ashes are washed
                            in the ides of the sea
And 'an astonished eye looks out of the air'
                    to see the poet singing there

And dusk falls down a coast somewhere

    where a white horse without a rider
            turns its head
                    to the sea

*First read at the City Lights Poets Theatre Kenneth Patchen
Memorial Reading, February 3, 1972, San Francisco*

AN IMAGINARY HAPPENING, LONDON

In the lower left-hand corner
of an album landscape
I am walking thru a dark park
with a noted nymphomaniac
trying to discover
for what she is noted

We are talking as we walk
of various villainies
of church & state
and of the tyrannies
of love & hate

The moon makes hairless nudes

An alabaster girl upon her back
becomes a body made of soap
beneath a wet gypsy

Suddenly we rush
thru a bent gate
into the hot grass

One more tree
falls in the forest

THOUGHTS TO A CONCERTO
OF TELEMANN

'The curious upward stumbling motion
of the oboe d'amore'
must be love itself among the strands
of emotion. It is as if its motion
were not its own at all,
as if these hands
had never struck those strings
we sing to,
swing to
(as puppets do, unbroken)
as if we never really meant to
be so strung to
those sweet pitches
love so frets us to
so tautly
so mutely
(love's bodies laid like harps!)
and then as if
there never were still more
unspoken,
as if dumb mind did never grieve
among the woodwinds,
as if its chords
did never quiver anymore
as in a buried mandolin,
as if that love
were hardly in it
anymore,
nor sounded in it

anymore,
nor heart hear it
nor life bear it
anymore.
Yet it does, it does!

TOC TOC: A COUPLE OBSERVED

(After Apollinaire)

Without closing its wings
                              the plane lands
                its shadow in mourning
                              for itself
            come down to itself on earth
Toc toc the clock in the tower continues
        to cast its shadow
                        onto the airfield
Toc toc another stroke of the feather
            strikes another line
                        in my face
        My shadow in mourning
                    for my self
                    tied to my feet
                    falls out of the plane
                    head first
                    ahead of my fate
Toc toc the shadows in the gardens of Père Lachaise
            draw over Apollinaire's tombeau
Toc toc the flowers of the garden are faded
        loose leaves & aeroplanes blow away
Toc toc another stroke of the feather
                    another line in a face
                a woman withdraws a man goes off
                    with his shadow
                    withdrawn into himself
                    Toc toc
                    they both turn
                    too late! too late!

POUND AT SPOLETO

I walked into a loge in the Teatro Melisso, the lovely Renaissance salle where the poetry readings and the chamber concerts were held every day of the Spoleto Festival, and suddenly saw Ezra Pound for the first time, still as a mandarin statue in a box in a balcony at the back of the theatre, one tier up from the stalls. It was a shock, seeing only a striking old man in a curious pose, thin and long haired, aquiline at 80, head tilted strangely to one side, lost in permanent abstraction. . . . After three younger poets on stage, he was scheduled to read from his box, and there he sat with an old friend (who held his papers) waiting. He regarded the knuckles of his hands, moving them a very little, expressionless. Only once, when everyone else in the full theatre applauded someone on stage, did he rouse himself to clap, without looking up, as if stimulated by sound in a void. . . . After almost an hour, his turn came. Or after a life. . . . Everyone in the hall rose, turned and looked back and up at Pound in his booth, applauding. The applause was prolonged and Pound tried to rise from his armchair. A microphone was partly in the way. He grasped the arms of the chair with his boney hands and tried to rise. He could not and he tried again and could not. His old friend did not try to help him. Finally she put a poem in his hand, and after at least a minute his voice came out. First the jaw moved and then the voice came out, inaudible. A young Italian pulled the mike up very close to his face and held it there and the voice came over, frail but stubborn, higher than I had expected, a thin, soft monotone. The hall had gone silent at a stroke. The voice knocked me down, so soft, so thin, so frail, so stubborn still. I put my head on my arms on the velvet sill of the box. I was surprised to see a single tear drop on my knee. The thin, indomitable voice went on. I went blind from the box, through the back door of it, into the empty corridor of the theatre where they still sat

117

turned to him, went down and out, into the sunlight, weep-
ing. . . .

Up above the town
                        by the ancient aqueduct
        the chestnut trees
                        were still in bloom
            Mute birds
                        flew in the valley
                                    far below
            The sun shone
                        on the chestnut trees
        and the leaves
                        turned in the sun
            and turned and turned and turned
                And would continue turning
        His voice
                    went on
                        and on
                            through the leaves. . . .

ON THE TRANSSIBERIAN

Knock knock on wooden Russia!
I am a white bird drilling holes
in the white wood of your snow.
To the white birches
that stretch across Siberia
from Vladivostok to Blok
I give one more knock.
Who will answer this time?
Are you still there, poet,
Are you still there, brother, anarchist,
Are you still there, under the plow?
These are not Chekhov's cherished cherry trees
that fell down long ago.
This is the eternal *taiga* now
that still stands up against all winds
dark scars upon the bark.

Knock! Knock!

Let the railsplitter
truly awake.

RECIPE FOR HAPPINESS IN KHABAROVSY OR ANYPLACE

One grand boulevard with trees
with one grand café in sun
with strong black coffee in very small cups

One not necessarily very beautiful
man or woman who loves you

One fine day

SALUTE

To every animal who eats or shoots his own kind
And every hunter with rifles mounted in pickup trucks
And every private marksman or minuteman
                              with telescopic sight
And every redneck in boots with dogs
                              & sawed-off shotguns
And every Peace Officer with dogs
                              trained to track & kill
And every plainclothesman or undercover agent
                  with shoulderholster full of death
And every servant of the people gunning down people
                  or shooting-to-kill fleeing felons
And every Guardia Civil in any country guarding civilians
                  with handcuffs & carbines
And every border guard at no matter what Check Point Charley
            on no matter which side of which Berlin Wall
                  Bamboo or Tortilla curtain
And every elite statetrooper highwaypatrolman in custom-
            tailored ridingpants & plastic crash helmet
            & shoestring necktie & sixshooter in silver-
            studded holster
And every prowlcar with riotguns & sirens and every riot-tank
            with mace & teargas
And every crackpilot with rockets & napalm underwing
And every skypilot blessing bombers at takeoff
And any State Department of any superstate selling guns
            to both sides
And every Nationalist of no matter what Nation in no matter
            what world Black Brown or White
                        who kills for his Nation

And every prophet or poet with gun or shiv and any enforcer
            of spiritual enlightenment with force and any
            enforcer of the power of any state with Power
And to any and all who kill & kill & kill & kill for Peace
I raise my middle finger
in the only proper salute

Santa Rita Prison, 1968

THIRD WORLD CALLING

This loud morning
        sensed a small cry in
        the news
                paper
           caught somewhere on
             an inner page
                    I
        decide to travel for lunch &
        end up in an automat
                White House Cafeteria
    looking thru a little window
      put a nickle in the slot
      and out comes
                fried rice
    Taking a tour
        of the rest of that building
      I hear a small cry
           beyond the rice paddies
                between floors where
                    the escalator sticks
  and remember last night's dream of
  attending my own funeral
    at a drive-in mortuary
      not really believing
           I was that dead
    Someone throwing rice
              All the windows dry
Tipped the coffin open & laughed
                  into it
      and out falls
             old funnyface
           myself

                    the bargain tragedian
          with a small cry
     followed by sound of Che Guevara singing
          in the voice of Fidel

Far over the Perfume River
                              the clouds pass
               carrying small cries
The monsoon has set in
                    the windows weep

          I
          back up to
                    the Pentagon
          on a flatbed truck
     and unload the small brown bodies
                    fresh from the blasted fields!

BASEBALL CANTO

Watching baseball
sitting in the sun
eating popcorn
reading Ezra Pound

and wishing Juan Marichal
would hit a hole right through
the Anglo-Saxon tradition
in the First Canto
and demolish the barbarian invaders

When the San Francisco Giants take the field
and everybody stands up to the National Anthem
with some Irish tenor's voice
piped over the loudspeakers
with all the players struck dead in their places
and the white umpires like Irish cops
in their black suits and little black caps
pressed over their hearts
standing straight and still
like at some funeral of a blarney bartender
and all facing East
as if expecting some Great White Hope
or the Founding Fathers
to appear on the horizon
like 1066 or 1776 or all that

But Willie Mays appears instead
in the bottom of the first
and a roar goes up
            as he clouts the first one into the sun
                  and takes off
                        like a footrunner from Thebes

The ball is lost in the sun
and maidens wail after him
but he keeps running
through the Anglo-Saxon epic

And Tito Fuentes comes up
looking like a bullfighter
in his tight pants and small pointed shoes

And the rightfield bleachers go mad
with chicanos & blacks & Brooklyn beerdrinkers
"Sweet Tito! Sock it to heem, Sweet Tito!"
And Sweet Tito puts his foot in the bucket
and smacks one that don't come back at all
and flees around the bases
like he's escaping from the United Fruit Company
as the gringo dollar beats out the Pound
and Sweet Tito beats it out
like he's beating out usury
not to mention fascism and anti-semitism

And Juan Marichal comes up
and the chicano bleachers go loco again
as Juan belts the first fast ball
out of sight
and rounds first and keeps going
and rounds second and rounds third
and keeps going
and hits pay-dirt
to the roars of the grungy populace
As some nut presses the backstage panic button
for the tape-recorded National Anthem again
to save the situation

but it don't stop nobody this time
in their revolution round the loaded white bases
in this last of the great Anglo-Saxon epics
in the *Territorio Libre* of baseball

LAUGHING & CRYING

I laugh to hear me say what I am saying

Walking in my cave of flesh

There must be a place

There must be a place

Where all is light

I laugh to hear me say what I am saying

O Rama

Audiart O Audiart

dancing Shiva dear one

Your face flies through the sky

I laugh to say what I am saying

Each of us a lamp

a spirit-lamp

a lantern burning

a lamp a place beyond a turning

where all is light

I laugh and cry

with mask of tears

and laughing face

I laugh and cry to hear me say what I am saying

My laughing face

and mask of tears

makes me laugh and cry to hear me sing what I am saying

For there must be a place

must be a place

where all is light

NIGHT LIGHT

Night, night
Death's true self, Death's second self
Black is my true love's hair
Yet all, all is despair

Black night, black light
Death's true self
Black, black, black is my true love's hair
And all, all is despair

Night, night
Death's second self
where all is empty, all is despair
All gone, all down
All, all despair
And grey is my true love's hair

Yet sun bursts forth upon the land
And a butterfly lights in it
upon my hand
And lights these songs
and lights these songs
in air

from Who Are We Now
1976

DIRECTOR OF ALIENATION

Looking in the mirrors at Macy's
and thinking it's a subterranean plot
to make me feel like Chaplin
snuck in with his bent shoes & beat bowler
looking for a fair-haired angel
Who's this bum
crept in off the streets
blinking in the neon
an anarchist among the floorwalkers
a strike-breaker even
right past the pickets
and the picket line is the People yet?
I think I'll hook a new derby
with my cane
and put a sign on it reading
Director of Alienation
or The Real Revolution
So it's Mister Alienation is it
like he don't like nobody?
It's not me It's Them out of step
I came in looking for an angel
male or female dark or fair
but why does everyone look
so serious or unhappy
like as if everyone's alienated
from something or someone
from the whole earth even
and the green land
among the loud indignant birds
My land is your land
but 'all is changed, changed utterly'

Look at this alien face
in this elevator mirror
The Tele-tector scans me
He looks paranoid Better get him out
before he starts trying on the underwear
Keep your filthy mitts offa
I better stick to the escalators
Too many nylon ladies in the lifts
too many two-way mirrors
I came in looking for an angel
among the alien corn
I might get caught
fingering the lingerie
feeling up the manikins
House dicks after me
Where's your credit cards
They'll find the hole in my sock
in the Shoe Department
The full-length mirrors all designed
to make you look your worst
so you'll get real depressed
and throw off your old clothes
and buy new duds on the spot
Well I'll take them at their word
They asked for it
Off with these grungy threads
and slide down the escalators bare-ass
Slip between the on-sale sheets
into the on-sale bed
feeling for an angel in it
Try this new flush toilet
and the portable shower
emerging from the bath in something sexy
into a store window
among the Coquette Wigs by Eva Gabor

and freeze in one of the wigs
when the Keystone Cops come running
I came in looking for an angel
passion eyes and longing hair
in mirrors made of water
But what's this wrack of civilization
I've fallen into
This must be the end of something
the last days of somebody's empire
Seven floors of it
from Women's Wear to Men's Furnishings
Lost souls descending thru
Dante's seven circles
Ladies like bees avaricious
clustered at counters
I don't want to join them either
Always the Outsider
What a drag
Why don't you get with it
It's your country
What a cliché this Outsider
a real bore
But is there anyone left inside
in this year of the boring Bicentennial
Indians alienated Artists alienated
All these poets alienated
Parents husbands wives alienated
Kids alienated
Even billionaires alienated
hiding out in foreign countries
Don't let them tell you different
with their flags and their grants
So Buy Buy Buy
and get Inside
Get a loada this junk

You wanna belong
You gotta have it
Pull yourself together
and descend to Macy's basement
And eat your way up
thru the seven stages
of this classless society
with the Credit Department on the top floor
where surely some revelation is at hand
Consume your way up
until you're consumed by it
at the very top
where surely a terrible beauty is born
Then jump off the roof
o dark of hair
o Ruth among the alien corn
waving plastic jewels and genitals

WILD DREAMS OF A NEW BEGINNING

There's a breathless hush on the freeway tonight
Beyond the ledges of concrete
restaurants fall into dreams
with candlelight couples
Lost Alexandria still burns
in a billion lightbulbs
Lives cross lives
idling at stoplights
Beyond the cloverleaf turnoffs
'Souls eat souls in the general emptiness'
A piano concerto comes out a kitchen window
A yogi speaks at Ojai
'It's all taking place in one mind'
On the lawn among the trees
lovers are listening
for the master to tell them they are one
with the universe
Eyes smell flowers and become them
There's a deathless hush
on the freeway tonight
as a Pacific tidal wave a mile high
                        sweeps in
Los Angeles breathes its last gas
and sinks into the sea like the *Titanic* all lights lit
Nine minutes later Willa Cather's Nebraska
                        sinks with it

The seas come in over Utah
Mormon tabernacles washed away like barnacles
Coyotes are confounded & swim nowhere
An orchestra onstage in Omaha
keeps on playing Handel's *Water Music*
Horns fill with water

and bass players float away on their instruments
clutching them like lovers horizontal
Chicago's Loop becomes a rollercoaster
Skyscrapers filled like water glasses
Great Lakes mixed with Buddhist brine
Great Books watered down in Evanston
Milwaukee beer topped with sea foam
Beau Fleuve of Buffalo suddenly become salt
Manhattan Island swept clean in sixteen seconds
buried masts of New Amsterdam arise
as the great wave sweeps on Eastward
to wash away over-age Camembert Europe
Mannahatta steaming in sea-vines
the washed land awakes again to wilderness
the only sound a vast thrumming of crickets
a cry of seabirds high over
in empty eternity
as the Hudson retakes its thickets
and Indians reclaim their canoes

LOST PARENTS

It takes a fast car
　　　　　　to lead a double life
in these days of short-distance love affairs
　　　when he has far-out lovers in
　　　　　　　　　three different locations
　　　and a date with each one
　　　　　　　　at least twice a week
　　　a little simple arithmetic shows
　　　　　　what a workout he's engaged in
crossing & recrossing the city
　　　　from bedroom to patio to swimming pool
the ignition key hot
　　　and the backseat a jumble of clothes
　　　　　　　　　　for different life-styles
　　　a surfboard on the roof
　　　and a copy of Kahlil Gibran or Rod McKuen
　　　　　　　　　under the dashboard
　　　　next to the Indian music casettes
　　packs of Tarot and the I-Ching
　　　　　　　crammed into the glove compartment
　　　along with old traffic tickets
　　　　　　　　and hardpacks of Kents
　　　dents attesting to the passion
　　　　　　　　　of his last lover
And his answering service
　　　catching him on the freeway
　　　　　　between two calls or two encounter groups
　　and the urgent message left
　　　with an unlisted number to call Carol
　　　about the bottle of fine wine
　　　　　he forgot to pick up
　　　　　and deliver to the gallery
　　　　　　　for the reception at nine

While she shuttles to her gynecologist
        and will meet him later
                between two other numbers
                            male or female
        including his wife
                who also called twice
wanting to know where he's been
        and what he's done
                    with their throw-away children
        who
                left to their own devices
                in a beach house at Malibu
        grew up and dropped out into Nothing
            in a Jungian search
                        for lost parents
                                their own age

PEOPLE GETTING DIVORCED

People getting divorced
        riding around with their clothes in the car
and wondering what happened
           to everyone and everything
          including their other
              pair of shoes
     And if you spy one
        then who knows what happened
              to the other
             with tongue alack
and years later not even knowing
          if the other ever
            found a mate
          without splitting the seams
          or remained intact
              unlaced
   and the sole
       ah the soul
           a curious conception
      hanging on somehow
           to walk again
              in the free air
         once the heel
             has been replaced

SHORT STORY ON A PAINTING OF GUSTAV KLIMT

They are kneeling upright on a flowered bed
  He
      has just caught her there
                  and holds her still
   Her gown
      has slipped down
                 off her shoulder
   He has an urgent hunger
          His dark head
             bends to hers
                hungrily
And the woman the woman
    turns her tangerine lips from his
        one hand like the head of a dead swan
        draped down over
               his heavy neck
       the fingers
          strangely crimped
             tightly together
     her other arm doubled up
          against her tight breast
     her hand a languid claw
             clutching his hand
     which would turn her mouth
               to his
    her long dress made
         of multicolored blossoms
         quilted on gold
    her Titian hair
        with blue stars in it

                And his gold
                        harlequin robe
                                checkered with
                                        dark squares
                Gold garlands
                        stream down over
                                her bare calves &
                                        tensed feet
Nearby there must be
                a jeweled tree
                        with glass leaves aglitter
                                in the gold air
It must be
                morning
                        in a faraway place somewhere
They
        are silent together
                                as in a flowered field
                        upon the summer couch
                                which must be hers
        And he holds her still
                        so passionately
                holds her head to his
                                so gently so insistently
                to make her turn
                                her lips to his
Her eyes are closed
                        like folded petals
She
        will not open
                        He
                        is not the One

ALIENATION: TWO BEES

I came upon them in the cabin—
the angry one at the window
and the old bent one on the bed
the one at the window buzzing & buzzing
beating its wings on the window
beating the pane
the one on the bed
the silent one with the bent frame
alone on the counterpane
I didn't mean to kill them
but the one in the window
wouldn't be waved
back to his hive
The door was open and he knew it
and flew in it for a moment
and then flew back
away from his community
Something had alienated him
and he would not go back
or was it perhaps
the wounded one on the bed
who kept him
I tried to get him to fasten onto
a crumpled page
of the local news
but he would not
And I must have hurt him doing that
for he fell on the bed
and died in an instant
stretching out his legs
or arms

as if to his comrade or lover
who crawled a quarter-inch toward him
and then hunched up
into a very small furry ball
and was still
and would not move again
As all at once outside
the hive hummed louder
with a million mild conformists
with wild antennas bent

Not one flew out to wake the dead

No messenger was sent

OLBERS' PARADOX

And I heard the learned astronomer
        whose name was Heinrich Olbers
   speaking to us across the centuries
    about how he observed with naked eye
     how in the sky there were
         some few stars close up
  and the further away he looked
      the more of them there were
  with infinite numbers of clusters of stars
     in myriad Milky Ways & myriad nebulae

So that from this we may deduce
    that in the infinite distances
        there must be a place
        there *must* be a place
          where all is light
  and that the light from that high place
          where all is light
     simply hasn't got here yet
     which is why we still have night

But when at last that light arrives
    when at last it does get here
       the part of day we now call Night
      will have a white sky
        with little black dots in it
        little black holes
          where once were stars
And then in that symbolic
     so poetic place
        which will be ours
   we'll be our own true shadows
    and our own illumination
            on a sunset earth

UPON REFLECTION

Night's black mirror is broken

  the star crab has scuttled away

     with the inkwell

       into India

  Dawn

       sows its mustard seed

In the steep ravines and gulches

       of Big Sur

  small animals stir

       under the tough underbrush

as sun creeps down the canyon walls

       into the narrow meadows

  where the wild quail

       run & cluck

  Daytime moon

  after much reflection says

       Sun is God

And the stream

  standing still

       rushes forward

DEEP CHESS

Life itself like championship chess
                          dark players jousting
               on a checkered field
                          where you have only
               so much time
                          to complete your moves
And your clock running
                          all the time
          and if you take
                          too much time
                                   for one move
          you have that much less
                                   for the rest
                          of your life
And your opponent
                    dark or fair
               (which may or may not be
                                   life itself)
bugging you with his deep eyes
     or obscenely wiggling his crazy eyebrows
     or blowing smoke in your face
          or crossing and recrossing his legs
                          or her legs
or otherwise screwing around
     and acting like some insolent invulnerable
                          unbeatable god
          who can read your mind & heart
And one hasty move
                    may ruin you
     for you must play
                    deep chess
          (like the one deep game Spassky won from Fisher)

148

And if your unstudied opening
                          was not too brilliant
      you must play to win not draw
        and suddenly come up with
                    a new Nabokov variation
And then lay Him out at last
        with some super end-game
                no one has ever even dreamed of

And there's still time—
                Your move

A MEETING OF EYES IN MEXICO

Suddenly
you are speaking to me
over the audience
as I speak my poem to it
My eyes encounter yours
over the crowd
Just a pair of eyes out there
in a far foto of faces
distant lamps
in a dark landscape
flickering
And the eyes speak—
in whatever tongue—
The poem ends
The eyes go on
burning
And there is applause out there
as on a dark sea
I hear it distantly
as in a sea shell—
shreds of sunlight blown—
As later your voice comes through—
in whatever tongue—
an impassioned questioning
of my poem—
I answer back
over the heads of the audience

I
  answer you
        Dark eyes
                speak to you
       over their heads
              Dark one
  'There is none
         like you
                among the dancers'

    Te amo

THE GENERAL SONG OF HUMANITY

On the coast of Chile where Neruda lived
it's well known that
seabirds often steal
letters out of mailboxes
which they would like to scan
for various reasons
Shall I enumerate the reasons?
They are quite clear
even given the silence of birds
on the subject
(except when they speak of it
among themselves
between cries)
First of all
they steal the letters because
they sense that the General Song
of the words of everyone
hidden in these letters
must certainly bear the keys
to the heart itself of humanity
which the birds themselves
have never been able to fathom
(in fact entertaining much doubt
that there actually are
hearts in humans)
And then these birds have a further feeling
that their own general song
might somehow be enriched
by these strange cries of humans
(What a weird bird-brain idea
that our titterings might enlighten them)

152

But when they stole away
              with Neruda's own letters
          out of his mailbox at Isla Negra
      they were in fact stealing back
              their own Canto General
      which he had originally gathered
                          from them
          with their omniverous & ecstatic
                          sweeping vision
But now that Neruda is dead
      no more such letters are written
          and they must play it by ear again—
          the high great song
                      in the heart of our blood & silence

Cuernavaca, October 26, '75

EIGHT PEOPLE ON A GOLF COURSE
AND ONE BIRD OF FREEDOM
FLYING OVER

The phoenix flies higher & higher
above eight elegant people on a golf course
who have their heads stuck in the sands
of a big trap
One man raises his head and shouts
I am President of Earth. I rule.
You elected me, heh-heh. Fore!
A second man raises his head.
I am King of the Car.
The car is my weapon. I drive all before me.
Ye shall have no other gods.
Watch out. I'm coming through.
A third raises his head out of the sand.
I run a religion. I am your spiritual head.
Never mind which religion.
I drive a long ball. Bow down and putt.
A fourth raises his head in the bunker.
I am the General. I have tanks to conquer deserts.
And my tank shall not want. I'm thirsty.
We play Rollerball. I love Arabs.
A fifth raises his head and opens his mouth.
I am Your Master's Voice.
I rule newsprint. I rule airwaves, long & short.
We bend minds. We make reality to order.
Mind Fuck Incorporated.
A sixth man raises his gold bald head.
I'm your friendly multinational banker.
I chew cigars rolled with petro-dollars.
We're above nations. We control the control.
I'll eat you all in the end.

I work on margins. Yours.
A woman raises her head higher than anyone.
I am the Little Woman. I'm the Tender Warrior
who votes like her husband. Who took my breasts.
A final figure rises, carrying all the clubs.
Stop or I'll shoot a hole-in-one.
I'm the Chief of All Police. I eat meat.
We know the enemy. You better believe it.
We're watching all you paranoids. Go ahead & laugh.
You're all in the computer. We've got all
your numbers. Except one
unidentified flying asshole.
On the radar screen.
Some dumb bird.
Every time I shoot it down
it rises.

POPULIST MANIFESTO

Poets, come out of your closets,
Open your windows, open your doors,
You have been holed-up too long
in your closed worlds.
Come down, come down
from your Russian Hills and Telegraph Hills,
your Beacon Hills and your Chapel Hills,
your Mount Analogues and Montparnasses,
down from your foot hills and mountains,
out of your tepees and domes.
The trees are still falling
and we'll to the woods no more.
No time now for sitting in them
As man burns down his own house
to roast his pig.
No more chanting Hare Krishna
while Rome burns.
San Francisco's burning,
Mayakovsky's Moscow's burning
the fossil-fuels of life.
Night & the Horse approaches
eating light, heat & power,
and the clouds have trousers.
No time now for the artist to hide
above, beyond, behind the scenes,
indifferent, paring his fingernails,
refining himself out of existence.
No time now for our little literary games,
no time now for our paranoias & hypochondrias,
no time now for fear & loathing,
time now only for light & love.

We have seen the best minds of our generation
destroyed by boredom at poetry readings.
Poetry isn't a secret society,
It isn't a temple either.
Secret words & chants won't do any longer.
The hour of *om*ing is over,
the time for keening come,
time for keening & rejoicing
over the coming end
of industrial civilization
which is bad for earth & Man.
Time now to face outward
in the full lotus position
with eyes wide open,
Time now to open your mouths
with a new open speech,
time now to communicate with all sentient beings,
All you 'Poets of the Cities'
hung in museums, including myself,
All you poet's poets writing poetry
about poetry,
All you poetry workshop poets
in the boondock heart of America,
All you house-broken Ezra Pounds,
All you far-out freaked-out cut-up poets,
All you pre-stressed Concrete poets,
All you cunnilingual poets,
All you pay-toilet poets groaning with graffitti,
All you A-train swingers who never swing on birches,
All you masters of the sawmill haiku
in the Siberias of America,
All you eyeless unrealists,
All you self-occulting supersurrealists,
All you bedroom visionaries
and closet agitpropagators,

All you Groucho Marxist poets
and leisure-class Comrades
who lie around all day
and talk about the workingclass proletariat,
All you Catholic anarchists of poetry,
All you Black Mountaineers of poetry,
All you Boston Brahmins and Bolinas bucolics,
All you den mothers of poetry,
All you zen brothers of poetry,
All you suicide lovers of poetry,
All you hairy professors of poesie,
All you poetry reviewers
drinking the blood of the poet,
All you Poetry Police—
Where are Whitman's wild children,
where the great voices speaking out
with a sense of sweetness and sublimity,
where the great new vision,
the great world-view,
the high prophetic song
of the immense earth
and all that sings in it
And our relation to it—
Poets, descend
to the street of the world once more
And open your minds & eyes
with the old visual delight,
Clear your throat and speak up,
Poetry is dead, long live poetry
with terrible eyes and buffalo strength.
Don't wait for the Revolution
or it'll happen without you,
Stop mumbling and speak out
with a new wide-open poetry
with a new commonsensual 'public surface'

with other subjective levels
or other subversive levels,
a tuning fork in the inner ear
to strike below the surface.
Of your own sweet Self still sing
yet utter 'the word en-masse'—
Poetry the common carrier
for the transportation of the public
to higher places
than other wheels can carry it.
Poetry still falls from the skies
into our streets still open.
They haven't put up the barricades, yet,
the streets still alive with faces,
lovely men & women still walking there,
still lovely creatures everywhere,
in the eyes of all the secret of all
still buried there,
Whitman's wild children still sleeping there,
Awake and walk in the open air.

from Northwest Ecolog
1978

THE OLD SAILORS

On the green riverbank
                    age late fifties
I am beginning
                    to remind myself
of my great Uncle Désir
                    in the Virgin Islands
On a Saint Thomas back beach
he lived when I last saw him
in a small shack
                    under the palms
Eighty years old
                    straight as a Viking
    (where the Danes once landed)
he stood looking out
                    over the flat sea
    blue eyes or grey
                    with the sea in them
salt upon his lashes
                    We
            were always sea wanderers
No salt here now
            by the great river
        in the high desert range
Old sailors stranded
            the steelhead
            they too lost without it
                            leap up and die

WILD LIFE CAMEO, EARLY MORN

By the great river Deschutes
                on the meadowbank greensward
        sun just hitting
                        the high bluffs
            stone cliffs sculpted
                            high away
                across the river

At the foot of a steep brown slope
                            a mile away
            six white-tail deer
        four young bucks with branched antlers
            and two small does
                            mute in eternity
                                drinking the river
    then in real time raising heads
        and climbing up and up
                            a steep faint switchback
                into full sun

I bring them close in the binoculars
                            as in a round cameo
        There is a hollow bole in a tree
                            one looks into
        One by one they
                    drink silence
                            (the two does last)
            one by one
                    climb up so calm
                        over the rim of the canyon
            and without looking back
                        disappear forever

    Like certain people
                    in my life

READING APOLLINAIRE BY
THE ROGUE RIVER

Reading Apollinaire here
sitting crosslegged
on sleepingbag & poncho
in the shadow of a huge hill
before the sun clears it
Woke up early on the shore
and heard the river shushing
(like the sound a snake might make
sliding over riprap
if you magnified the sound)
My head still down upon the ground
one eye without perspective
sees the stream sliding by
through the sand
as in a desert landscape
Like a huge green watersnake
with white water markings
the river slithers by
and where the canyon turns
and the river drops from sight
seems like a snake about to disappear
down a deep hole
Indians made their myths
of this great watersnake
slid down from mountains far away
And I see the Rogue for real
as the Indians saw him
the Rogue all wild white water
a cold-blooded creature
drowning and dousing
the Rogue ruler of the land
transforming it at will
with a will of its own

a creature to be feared and respected
pillaging its way to the sea
with great gravity
still ruled by that gravity
which still rules all
so that we might almost say
Gravity is God
manifesting Himself
as Great God Sun
who will one day make Himself
into a black hole in space
who will one day implode Himself
into Nothing
All of which the slithering Rogue
knows nothing of
in its headlong
blind rush to the sea
And though its head
is already being eaten
by that most cruel and churning
monster Ocean
the tail of the snake
knows it not
and continues turning & turning
toward its final hole
and toward that final black hole
into which all some day
will be sucked burning

As I sit reading a French poet
    whose most famous poem is about
        the river that runs through the city
            taking time & life & lovers with it
            And none returning
                    none returning

HORSES AT DAWN

The horses the horses the wild horses at dawn
as in a watercolor by Ben Shahn
they are alive in the high meadow
in the high country on the far mesa
you can see them galloping
you can see them snorting
you can hear their thunder distantly
you can hear the small thunder
of their small hooves
insistently
like wood hammers thrumming
on a distant drum
The sun roars &
throws their shadows
out of the night

INTO THE DEEPER POOLS . . .

I put on the diving mask and went down / A few feet below the surface a few minnows circled me / A little further down a few small trout no more than three inches / I lie motionless just below the surface and search the deepest part of the pool / There at the very bottom between boulders / in the very deepest hole / I suddenly spy him / a huge fat grey speckled trout / perhaps eight pounds / perfectly still against the grey rocks / He would have been invisible from the surface / and invisible without the mask / Then suddenly I see another fat speckled trout / not quite as big / quite close to the first / almost like his shadow / or her shadow / this one too perfectly motionless / as if not even breathing / though the swift stream poured by above it / Summer of the great drought / and this the only deep pool left / the stream itself shrunk to a width of twenty feet / The pool isolated by rapids at each end / Last season the two fish must have made it up this far / then the stream shrunk still more / and here they were caught / in the shrinking hole / where they lay motionless / waiting / trapped / their world shrinking and shrinking / Still they lie at the bottom / very still / conserving what they've got / Fishermen don't have divingmasks and never see them down there and pass on quickly / as we dive down again & again / and see the fish in their steady-state of meditation / a final yoga discipline / which could go on until there is no water at all left in the stream / Then we might find them / still in swimming position / fins extended / mouth slightly open / eyes half closed / Or still later we might find their skeletons intact / in the same positions / baked in the firey sun / like Buddhist monks burned alive in lotus positions / Or still much later another age might discover / two fossil skeletons / imprinted on the boulders / at the very bottom of the crypt / as evidence of some former strange form / of a thing called Life / And if we stayed on here with them / waiting & waiting / that later age / might also not be able to imagine one boy and his father fishing / by this stream / though our two round skulls be found / with the fishes / Yet seeing now the beauty of those fish / down there below the surface / so still and lovely / in their deep dream / dappled in their last deep pool / We fish no longer / turn / and go on / into the deeper pools / of our own lives.

ROUGH SONG OF ANIMALS DYING

In a dream within a dream I dreamt a dream
of the reality of existence
inside the ultimate computer
which is the universe
in which the Arrow of Time
flies both ways
through bent space
In a dream within a dream I dreamt a dream
of all the animals dying
all animals everywhere
dying & dying
the wild animals the longhaired animals
winged animals feathered animals
clawed & scaled & furry animals
rutting & dying & dying
In a dream within a dream I dreamt a dream
of creatures everywhere dying out
in shrinking rainforests
in piney woods & high sierras
on shrinking prairies & tumbleweed mesas
captured beaten strapped starved & stunned
cornered & traded
species not meant to be nomadic
wandering rootless as man
In a dream within a dream I dreamt a dream
of all the animals crying out
in their hidden places
in the still silent places left to them
slinking away & crawling about
through the last wild places
through the dense underbrush
the last Great Thickets
beyond the mountains

crisscrossed with switchbacks
beyond the marshes
beyond the plains & fences
(the West won with barbed-wire machines)
in the high country
in the low country
crisscrossed with highways
In a dream within a dream I dreamt a dream
of how they feed & rut & run & hide
In a dream within a dream I saw
how the seals are beaten on the ice-fields
the soft white furry seals with eggshell skulls
the Great Green turtles beaten & eaten
exotic birds netted & caged & tethered
rare wild beasts & strange reptiles & weird woozoos
hunted down for zoos
by bearded blackmarketeers
who afterwards ride around Singapore
in German limousines
In a dream within a dream I dreamt a dream
of the earth heating up & drying out
in the famous Greenhouse Effect
under its canopy of carbon dioxide
breathed out by a billion
infernal combustion engines
mixed with the sweet smell of burning flesh
In a dream within a dream I dreamt a dream
of animals calling to each other
in codes we never understand
The seal and steer cry out
in the same voice
as they are clubbed
in Chicago stockyards & Newfoundland snowfields
It is the same cry
The wounds never heal

in the commonweal of animals
We steal their lives
to feed our own
and with their lives
our dreams are sown
In a dream within a dream I dreamt a dream
of the daily scrimmage for existence
in the wind-up model of the universe
the spinning meat-wheel world
in which I was a fish who eats his tail
in which I was a claw upon a beach
in which I was a snake upon a tree
in which I was a serpent's egg
a yin-yang yolk of good and evil
about to consume itself

from Landscapes of Living & Dying
1979

THE OLD ITALIANS DYING

For years the old Italians have been dying
all over America
For years the old Italians in faded felt hats
have been sunning themselves and dying
You have seen them on the benches
in the park in Washington Square
the old Italians in their black high button shoes
the old men in their old felt fedoras
                    with stained hatbands
have been dying and dying
                    day by day
You have seen them
every day in Washington Square San Francisco
the slow bell
tolls in the morning
in the Church of Peter & Paul
in the marzipan church on the plaza
toward ten in the morning the slow bell tolls
in the towers of Peter & Paul
and the old men who are still alive
sit sunning themselves in a row
on the wood benches in the park
and watch the processions in an out
funerals in the morning
weddings in the afternoon
slow bell in the morning Fast bell at noon
In one door out the other
the old men sit there in their hats
and watch the coming & going
You have seen them
the ones who feed the pigeons
                    cutting the stale bread
                        with their thumbs & penknives

the ones with old pocketwatches
the old ones with gnarled hands
                        and wild eyebrows
the ones with the baggy pants
                        with both belt & suspenders
the grappa drinkers with teeth like corn
the Piemontesi the Genovesi the Sicilianos
                        smelling of garlic & pepperonis
the ones who loved Mussolini
the old fascists
the ones who loved Garibaldi
the old anarchists reading *L' Umanita Nova*
the ones who loved Sacco & Vanzetti
They are almost all gone now
They are sitting and waiting their turn
and sunning themselves in front of the church
over the doors of which is inscribed
a phrase which would seem to be unfinished
from Dante's *Paradiso*
about the glory of the One
                        who moves everything . . .
The old men are waiting
for it to be finished
for their glorious sentence on earth
                        to be finished
the slow bell tolls & tolls
the pigeons strut about
not even thinking of flying
the air too heavy with heavy tolling
The black hired hearses draw up
the black limousines with black windowshades
shielding the widows
the widows with the long black veils
who will outlive them all
You have seen them

madre di terra, madre di mare
The widows climb out of the limousines
The family mourners step out in stiff suits
The widows walk so slowly
up the steps of the cathedral
fishnet veils drawn down
leaning hard on darkcloth arms
Their faces do not fall apart
They are merely drawn apart
They are still the matriarchs
outliving everyone
the old dagos dying out
in Little Italys all over America
the old dead dagos
hauled out in the morning sun
that does not mourn for anyone
One by one Year by year
they are carried out
The bell
never stops tolling
The old Italians with lapstrake faces
are hauled out of the hearses
by the paid pallbearers
in mafioso mourning coats & dark glasses
The old dead men are hauled out
in their black coffins like small skiffs
They enter the true church
for the first time in many years
in these carved black boats
                    ready to be ferried over
The priests scurry about
                as if to cast off the lines
The other old men
                        still alive on the benches
watch it all with their hats on

You have seen them sitting there
waiting for the bocci ball to stop rolling
waiting for the bell
                to stop tolling & tolling
for the slow bell
          to be finished tolling
telling the unfinished *Paradiso* story
as seen in an unfinished phrase
              on the face of a church
as seen in a fisherman's face
in a black boat without sails
making his final haul

THE SEA AND OURSELVES
AT CAPE ANN

Caw Caw Caw
on a far shingle long ago
when as a boy I came here
put ear to shell
>> of the thundering sea
>>>> sundering sea
>> seagulls high over
>>>> calling & calling
>> back then
>>>> at Cape Ann Gloucester
Where Olson saw himself Ishmael
and wrote his own epitaph:
>> 'I set out now
>>>> in a box upon the sea'
And Creeley found his creel
>> yet would not / cd. not
>>>> speak of the sea
And Ferrini took the wind's clothes
>> and became the conscience of Gloucester
Yet none could breathe
>> a soul into the sea
And I saw the tide pools gasping
>> the sea's mouth roaring
>>>> polyphoboistrous
>> beyond the Ten Pound Light
>>>> roistering
>>>> off far islands
Where Eliot heard
>> the sea's stark meditation
>> off *beauport* Gloucester

Where I as a man much later
                    made a landfall in the gloaming
          sighting from seaward in convoy
                         beyond the gulls' far off
                                        tattered cries
               cats' cries lost
                    reached to us
                              in shredded snatches
          Then as now
Eliot must
               have been a seaman
                         in his city soul
     to have heard so deeply
                    the sea's voice sounding then
                         in 'The Dry Salvages'
Here now
          where now
                    is the sea's urge still
          sea's surge and thunder
                              except within us
                    folded under
     by the beach road now
                         rapt in darkness
The sea still a great door never opened
               great ships asunder
                         clinker-built bottoms
               nets hung with cork
                    hulls heavy with caulking
While still the Nor'easter blows
               still the high tides
                    seethe & sweep shoreward
     batter the breakwaters
                    the granite harbors
                              rock villages
          Land's End lashed again
                         in 'the sudden fury'

And still the stoned gulls soaring over
                    crying & calling & crying
          blissed-out up there
                         in the darkening air
          over the running sea
                    the runing sea
               over dark stone beach under stars
Where now we sit
               'distracted from distraction' still
     Odyssey turned to *Iliad*
                         in parked cars

A SWEET FLYING DREAM

We were two naked
                light-headed dandelions
                                with natural hair blown out
                floating high over the landscape
                                blown by zephyr winds
                our long legs dangling
                                        straight down
                                translucent
                                        dandelion stems
                in an archetypal primordial dream
                                        of flying
Sweet hills & waters
                        flowed below us
                as we floated high over
                                lakes & rivers
                                        & windblown peaks
We
    drifted
            wafted easily
                            We
                                flew wingless
        Full of air
                    our hair
                            buoyed us
    We
        trailed our slim legs
                            in streams of silver air
                    There
                        was nothing
                                blowing us down
                                or away
                                    from each other

After a long way
              and a long while
                         we
                             glided down
                   lower & lower
     in great swinging circles
         The sea
              the lapping sea
                     rose up
   and we
          were over
              dry gold land
                   close up
and I
     I was afraid you would
               come against the ground too hard
   and I reached down
             and took
               your two extended hands
                     in mine
   and held you below me
           like that
               floating
As we drifted
        lower & lower
    the earth
        came up to us
            so softly
And
   we landed
       so quietly
    sank
     so gently
        to the bright soft ground
And lay in the light
       flowerless fields

TWO SCAVENGERS IN A TRUCK,
TWO BEAUTIFUL PEOPLE IN A
MERCEDES

At the stoplight waiting for the light
                    Nine A.M. downtown San Francisco
    a bright yellow garbage truck
                    with two garbagemen in red plastic blazers
        standing on the back stoop
                            one on each side hanging on
        and looking down into
                            an elegant open Mercedes
                with an elegant couple in it
The man
        in a hip three-piece linen suit
            with shoulder-length blond hair & sunglasses
The young blond woman so casually coifed
                    with a short skirt and colored stockings
        on the way to his architect's office

And the two scavengers up since Four A.M.
                            grungy from their route
                on the way home
The older of the two with grey iron hair
                            and hunched back
            looking down like some
                            gargoyle Quasimodo
And the younger of the two
                        also with sunglasses & longhair
        about the same age as the Mercedes driver

And both scavengers gazing down
                            as from a great distance
                at the cool couple

as if they were watching some odorless TV ad
               in which everything is always possible

And the very red light for an instant
              holding all four close together
      as if anything at all were possible
                          between them
     across that great gulf
                in the high seas
                        of this democracy

THE BILLBOARD PAINTERS

The two
           white-overalled white-capped
                                         signpainters
                        on the high
                                    scaffold suspended
                        on the huge
                                    billboard
                                beside the elevated
                                                   freeway
           painting a snapshot landscape of
                                    a South Sea island beach
                        with lagoon and coral reef and
                                                        palmtrees
                              thru which the sun
                                             is setting and
the two
           white painters painting a
                                       sunburned
                              North American couple on the
                                                        white beach
              and the real sun cold
                        over the myriad flashing cars in
                              the middle of San Francisco
                        next to the Hall of questionmark
                                                   Justice and
the two
           all-white painters
                             struck motionless with
              arms and paintbrushes raised
                                    halfway thru the
                                      landscape with
                        the right half painted and

the left half still blank
white on white as if
the other half of the world had
still to be provided for
or as if
God or some other
slightly less omnipotent
Creator was maybe
changing his or her mind half-
way thru as if
even he or she was
not so certain anymore it
was such a good idea after
all
to have
these two so-white All American
painters painting
that paradise on earth
as if
the advertisers who
were paying for this sign
hadn't already recycled that
particular paradise
with a jet strip and
hotels looking like the
American
roman empire where
they had to advertise now in
order to fill those fancy
wateringplaces with
retired billboard
painters who
belonged to the union and
got themselves and their wives
all these
benefits like

                    South Sea island trips after
                        working all their lives in
                        untropical places like
                                        San Francisco
                                        which
Sir Francis Drake found and
                    wrote back to the head of *his*
                            empire saying he
                had just discovered
                                    a real unspoiled
                                    native paradise and
                    if they hurried and
                      put up billboards back home they
                        might just be able to
                            set up a colony out
                            here with
                    swimming pools and even maybe make
                a pot of gold or
                                    a killing and
                    die happy in
                                a beach chair
                        very far
                            from home

HOME HOME HOME

Where are they going
all these brave intrepid animals
Fur and flesh
in steel cabinets
on wheels
high-tailing it
Four PM Friday freeway
over the hidden land
San Francisco's burning
with the late sun
in a million windows
The four-wheeled animals
are leaving it to burn
They're escaping
almost flying
home to the nest
home to the warm caves
in the hidden hills & valleys
home to daddy home to mama
home to the little wonders
home to the pot plants behind the garage
The cars the painted cabinets
streak for home home home
THRU TRAFFIC MERGE LEFT
home to the hidden turning
the hidden yearning
home to San Jose
home to Santa Cruz & Monterey
home to Hamilton Avenue
home to the Safeway the safest way
YIELD
LEFT LANE MUST TURN LEFT

home to the little grey home in the West
home to Granddaddy on the golfcourse
home to Uncle Ned
puttering in the toolshed
having lost his pants
on the stock exchange
home to big sister
who lost her way in encounter groups
home to the 97-1b housewife
driving two tons of chrome & steel
three blocks to the supermarket
to buy a package of baby pins
home to little sister
blushing with boyfriends
in the laundryroom
home to kid brother with skateboards & Adidas
home to mad Uncle building CB radios
in hidden bunkers
home to backyard barbecues
with aerospace neighbors
Mr. Wilson's coming over
The Hendersons will all be there
Home to Hidden Valley
where the widow waits
by the Cross on the mountain
where hangs the true madness
home to Santa's Village
WILL DIVIDE TO SUIT
GAS FOOD LODGING NEXT RIGHT
home to where the food is
home to Watsonville
home to Salinas
past the Grapes of Wrath
past United Farmworkers

stooped over artichokes
home home over the horizon
where the sun still blows
into the sea
home to Big Sur
and the garden of delights
and the oranges of Hieronymous Bosch
the sun still sets
in lavender skies
Home sweet home the salesman sighs
home safe at home in the bathroom
safe with the washingmachine & dishwasher
safe with the waterheater
safe with the kitchen clock
tick tick
the time is not yet
the alarm is set
safe at last in the double bed
hidden from each other
in the dark bed by the winding stair
the enchanted place in the still air
hidden each from each
or the queensize bed the kingsize bed
the waterbed with the vibrator
with the nylon nympho in it
the bed of roses
the bed with Big Emma in it
with the stoned-out Angel in it
(Mountains of flesh
Hills of hips & thighs
Rolling landscapes of heaving meat
Groans & moans & cries!)
Home to the bed we made
and must lie in

with 'whoever'
Or home to the bed still to be made
of ragas & visions
the bed whose form is pure light
(and unheard melodies
dark despairs & inchoate ecstasies
longings out of reach)
Who to decipher them who answer them
singing each to each?
Hidden from themselves
The beds are warm with them
The springs quake
on the San Andreas Fault
The dark land broods
Look in my eye, look in my eye
the cyclope tv cries
It blinks and rolls its glassy eye
and shakes its vacuum head
over the shaken bodies
in the bed

SAN JOSE SYMPHONY RECEPTION

(*Flagrante delicto*)

The bald man in plaid playing the harpsichord
    stopped short and sidled over
                   to the sideboard
      and copped a piece of Moka
             on a silver plate
      and slid back and started playing again
        some kind of Hungarian rhapsodate
    while the lady with the green eyeshades
        leaned over him exuding
               admiration & lust
Half notes danced & tumbled
             out of his instrument
      exuding a faint odor of
          chocolate cake
In the corner I was taking
        a course in musical destruction
  from the dark lady cellist
    who bent over me with her bow unsheathed
      and proceeded to saw me in half
As a consequence my pants fell right off
   revealing a badly bent trombone which
    even the first flutist
      who had perfect embouchure
           couldn't straighten out

WHITE ON WHITE

Today I'll write white on white
wear nothing but white
drink nothing but white
eat nothing but white
And I would be that sea-creature
who eats light
straining the ocean for its phosphorous—
For present time
is a 'white dot' in space
and white is the sand
in the hourglass
running out
White dunes of Africa
running through it
Snows of Siberia
sifting through it
The seas white with sperm
under the white moon
where aluminum stars wheel about
noiselessly
over quivering earth
with its white whales
white phagocytes
white bleached skulls
and albino animals
(Blacks bleached out
into white men?)
And to dream of white string
a symbol of innocence
Though the color of death be white
And the world checkered with death
white-on-black & black-on-white

'dumb pawns
in black-and-white kingdoms'
An angel stands on a station platform
slowly shaking its gossamer wings
A white horse
comes alone from a torn village
Everywhere around the earth
on station platforms they
are still putting up the placards
No pasaran
Go back Wrong way
White searchlights
search the sky
The gun turrets turn
on the old Walls
The angel slowly moves its wings
breathing the light white air
The earth breathes and trembles with it
The governed
will be governed
Liberty is not freedom
Eros versus civilization
No Way
without a pass
It is snowing white documents
The very rich
get richer still
A white gloved hand
still reaches out the window
for the money in the cup
Liberty is not free
The angel
stands on the edge
of the station platform

slowly moving its large white wings
which look too fragile
to lift the body of being
which still breathes anarchist air
And the train
the train made of nothing but boxcars
jammed with three billion people
still stands in the station trembling
And white phoenixes arise
out of piñon smoke
And the 'white sphinx of chance'
still holds its tongue
on the desert roads of the future

AN ELEGY TO DISPEL GLOOM

(After the assassinations of Mayor George Moscone and Supervisor Harvey Milk in San Francisco, November, 1978)

Let us not sit upon the ground
and tell sad stories
of the death of sanity.
Two humans made of flesh
are meshed in death
and no more need be said.
It is pure vanity
to think that all humanity
be bathed in red
because one young mad man
one so bad man
lost his head.
The force that through the red fuze
drove the bullet
does not drive everyone
through the City of Saint Francis
where there's a breathless hush
in the air today
a hush at City Hall
and a hush at the Hall of Justice
a hush in Saint Francis Wood
where no bird
tries to sing
a hush on the Great Highway
and in the great harbor
upon the great ships
and on the Embarcadero
from the Mission Rock Resort
to the Eagle Cafe

a hush on the great red bridge
and on the great grey bridge
a hush in the Outer Mission
and at Hunter's Point
a hush at a hot potato stand on Pier 39
and a hush at the People's Temple
where no bird
tries its wings
a hush and a weeping
at the Convent of the Sacred Heart
on Upper Broadway
a hush upon the fleshpots
of Lower Broadway
a pall upon the punk rock
at Mabuhay Gardens
and upon the cafes and bookstores
of old North Beach
a hush upon the landscape
of the still wild West
where two sweet dudes are dead
and no more need be said.
Do not sit upon the ground and speak
of other senseless murderings
or worse disasters waiting
in the wings
Do not sit upon the ground and talk
of the death of things beyond
these sad sad happenings.
Such men as these do rise above
our worst imaginings.

ADIEU À CHARLOT
(*Second Populist Manifesto*)

Sons of Whitman sons of Poe
sons of Lorca & Rimbaud
or their dark daughters
poets of another breath
poets of another vision
Who among you still speaks of revolution
Who among you still unscrews
the locks from the doors
in this revisionist decade?
'You are President of your own body, America'
Thus spoke Kush in Tepotzlan
youngblood wildhaired angel poet
one of a spawn of wild poets
in the image of Allen Ginsberg
wandering the wilds of America
'You Rimbauds of another breath'
sang Kush
and wandered off with his own particular paranoias
maddened like most poets
for one mad reason or another
in the unmade bed of the world
Sons of Whitman
in your 'public solitude'
bound by blood-duende
'President of your own body America'
Take it back from those who have maddened you
back from those who stole it
and steal it daily
The subjective must take back the world
from the objective gorillas & guerrillas of the world
We must rejoin somehow

the animals in the fields
in their steady-state meditation
'Your life is in your own hands still
Make it flower make it sing'
(so sang mad Kush in Tepotzlan)
'a constitutional congress of the body'
still to be convened to seize control
of the State
the subjective state
from those who have subverted it
The arab telephone of the avant-garde
has broken down
And I speak to you now
from another country
Do not turn away
in your public solitudes
you poets of other visions
of the separate lonesome visions
untamed uncornered visions
fierce recalcitrant visions
you Whitmans of another breath
which is not the too-cool breath of modern poetry
which is not the halitosis of industrial civilization
Listen now Listen again
to the song in the blood the dark duende a dark singing
between the tickings of civilization
between the lines of its headlines
in the silences between cars
driven like weapons
In two hundred years of freedom
we have invented
the permanent alienation of the subjective
almost every truly creative being
alienated & expatriated
in his own country

in Middle America or San Francisco
the death of the dream in your birth
o meltingpot America
I speak to you
from another country
another kind of blood-letting land
from Tepotzlan the poets' lan'
Land of the Lord of the Dawn

                         Quetzalcoatl

Land of the Plumed Serpent
I signal to you
as Artaud signaled
through the flames
I signal to you
over the heads of the land
the hard heads that stand like menhirs
above the land in every country
the short-haired hyenas
who still rule everything
I signal to you from Poets' Land
you poets of the alienated breath
to take back your land again
and the deep sea of the subjective
Have you heard the sound of the ocean lately
the sound by which daily
the stars still are driven
the sound by which nightly
the stars retake their sky
The sea thunders still to remind you
of the thunder in the blood
to remind you of your selves
Think now of your self
as of a distant ship
Think now of your beloved
of the eyes of your beloved

201

whoever is most beloved
he who held you hard in the dark
or she who washed her hair by the waterfall
whoever makes the heart pound
the blood pound
Listen says the river
Listen says the sea Within you
you with your private visions
of another reality a separate reality
Listen and study the charts of time
Read the sanskrit of ants in the sand
You Whitmans of another breath
there is no one else to tell
how the alienated generations
have lived out their expatriate visions
here and everywhere
The old generations have lived them out
Lived out the bohemian myth in Greenwich Villages
Lived out the Hemingway myth
in *The Sun Also Rises*
at the Dôme in Paris
or with the bulls at Pamplona
Lived out the Henry Miller myth
in the *Tropics* of Paris
and the great Greek dream
of *The Colossus of Maroussi*
and the tropic dream of Gauguin
Lived out the D. H. Lawrence myth
in *The Plumed Serpent*
in Mexico Lake Chapala
And the Malcolm Lowry myth
Under the Volcano at Cuernavaca
And then the saga of *On the Road*
and the Bob Dylan myth Blowing in the Wind
How many roads must a man walk down

How many Neal Cassadys on lost railroad tracks
How many replicas of Woody Guthrie with cracked guitars
How many photocopies of longhaired Joan
How many Ginsberg facsimiles and carbon-copy Keseys
still wandering the streets of America
in old tennis shoes and backpacks
or driving beat-up school buses
with destination-signs reading 'Further'
How many Buddhist Catholics how many cantors
chanting the Great Paramita Sutra
on the Lower East Side
How many Whole Earth Catalogs
lost in out-houses on New Mexico communes
How many Punk Rockers waving swastikas
Franco is dead but so is Picasso
Chaplin is dead but I'd wear his bowler
having outlived all our myths but his
the myth of the pure subjective
the collective subjective
the Little Man in each of us
waiting with Charlot or Pozzo
On every corner I see them
hidden inside their tight clean clothes
Their hats are not derbys they have no canes
but we know them
we have always
waited with them
They turn and hitch their pants
and walk away from us
down the darkening road
in the great American night

(Tepotzlan '75—San Francisco '78)

Work-in-Progress

RETIRED BALLERINAS,
CENTRAL PARK WEST

Retired ballerinas on winter afternoons
    walking their dogs
          in Central Park West
     (or their cats on leashes—
        the cats themselves old highwire artists)
The ballerinas
      leap and pirouette
          through Columbus Circle
    while winos on park benches
       (laid back like drunken Goudonovs)
    hear the taxis trumpet together
      like horsemen of the apocalypse
         in the dusk of the gods
It is the final witching hour
      when swains are full of swan songs
And all return through the dark dusk
    to their bright cells
        in glass highrises
   or sit down to oval cigarettes and cakes
         in the Russian Tea Room
   or climb four flights to back rooms
         in Westside brownstones
     where faded playbill photos
       fall peeling from their frames
        like last year's autumn leaves

MODERN POETRY IS PROSE
(BUT IT IS SAYING PLENTY)

I am thumbing through a great anthology of contemporary poetry, and it would seem that "the voice that is great within us" sounds within us mostly in a prose voice, albeit in the typography of poetry. Which is not to say it is prosaic or has no depths, which is not to say it is dead or dying, or not lovely or not beautiful or not well written or not witty and brave. It is very much alive, very well written, lovely, lively prose—prose that stands without the crutches of punctuation, prose whose syntax is so clear it can be written all over the page, in open forms and open fields, and still be very clear, very dear prose. And in the typography of poetry, the poetic and the prosaic intellect masquerade in each other's clothes.

Walking through our prose buildings in the 21st century, one may look back and wonder at this strange age which allowed poetry to walk in prose rhythms and still called it poetry. Modern poetry is prose because it sounds as subdued as any city man or woman whose life force is submerged in urban life. Modern poetry is prose because it has no *duende*, dark spirit of earth and blood, no soul of dark song, no passion musick. Like modern sculpture, it loves the concrete. Like minimal art, it minimizes emotion in favor of understated irony and implied intensity. As such it is the perfect poetry for technocratic man. But how often does this poetry rise above the mean sea level of his sparkling plain? Ezra Pound once decanted his opinion that only in times of decadence does poetry separate itself from music. And this is the way the world ends, not with a song but a whimper.

Eighty or ninety years ago, when all the machines began to hum, almost (as it seemed) in unison, the speech of man certainly began to be affected by the absolute staccato of machines. And city poetry certainly echoed it. Whitman was a holdover, singing the song of himself. And Sandburg a holdover, singing his sagas. And Vachel Lindsay a holdover, drumming his chants. And later there was Wallace Stevens with his harmonious "fictive music." And there was Langston Hughes. And Allen Ginsberg, chanting his mantras, singing Blake. There still are others everywhere, jazz poets and poetic strummers and wailers in the streets of the world, making poetry out of the urgent insurgent Now, of the immediate instant self, the incarnate carnal self (as D. H. Lawrence called it).

But much poetry was caught up in the linotype's hot slug and now in the so cold type of IBM. No song among the typists, no song in our concrete architecture, our concrete music. And the nightingales may still be singing near the Convent of the Sacred Heart, but we can hardly hear them in the city waste lands of T. S. Eliot, nor in his *Four Quartets* (which can't be played on any instrument and yet is the most beautiful prose of our time). Nor in the prose wastes of Ezra Pound's *Cantos* which aren't *canti* because they can't be sung by anyone. Nor in the pangolin prose of Marianne Moore (who called her writing poetry for lack of anything better to call it). Nor in the great prose blank verse of Karl Shapiro's *Essay on Rime*, nor in the inner city speech of William Carlos Williams, in the flat-out speech of his *Paterson*. All of which is applauded by poetry professors and poetry reviewers in all the best places, none of whom will commit the original sin of saying some poet's poetry is prose in the typography of poetry—just as the poet's friends will never tell him, just as the poet's editors will never say it—the dumbest conspiracy of silence in the history of letters.

Most modern poetry is poetic prose but it is saying plenty, by its own example, about what death of the spirit our technocratic civilization may be dealing us, enmeshed in machines and macho nationalisms, while we continue longing for the nightingale among the pines of Respighi. It is the bird singing that makes us happy.

ENDLESS LIFE

Endless the splendid life of the world
Endless its lovely living and breathing
its lovely sentient beings
seeing and hearing feeling and thinking
laughing and dancing sighing and crying
through endless afternoons endless nights
of love and ecstasy joy and despair
drinking and doping talking and singing
in endless Amsterdams of existence
with endless lively conversations
over endless cups of coffee
in literary cafes on rainy mornings
Endless street movies passing
in cars and trams of desire
on the endless tracks of light
And endless longhair dancing
to airless punk rock and airhead disco
through Milky Way midnights
to the Paradisos of dawn
talking and smoking and thinking
of everything endless at night
in the white of night the light of night
Ah yes oh yes the endless living and loving
hating and loving kissing and killing
Endless the ticking breathing breeding
meat-wheel of life
turning on and on through time
Endless life and endless death
endless air and endless breath
Endless worlds without end of days
in autumn capitals
their avenues of leaves ablaze

Endless dreams and sleep unravelling
the knitted sleeves of care
the labyrinths of thought
the labyrêves of love
the coils of desire and longing
myriad endgames of the unnameable
Endless the heavens on fire
endless universe spun out
World upon a mushroom pyre
Endless the fire that breathes in us
tattood fire-eaters dancing in plazas
swallowing flaming gasoline air
Brave the beating heart of flaming life
its beating and pulsings and flame-outs
Endless the open fields of the senses
the smell of lust and love
the calling and calling of cats in heat
their scent of must of musk
No end to the sound of the making of love
to the sound of bed springs creaking
to the moan of lovers making it
heard through the wall at night
No end to their groans of ecstasy
moans of the last lost climax
the sound of jukebox jumping
the flow of jass and gyzm
jived in Paradiso
And then the endless attempts to escape
the *nausée* of Sartre
the bald hills of burned out sensation
joie de vivre in despair
boatloads of enlightenment
ships of *merde* afloat by Charon's moat
greeds hysterias paranoias
pollutions and perversions
Endless *l'homme revolté*

in the anonymous face of death
in the tracks of the monster state
Endless his anarchist visions
endless his alienation
endless his alienated poetry
gadfly of the state Bearer of Eros
Endless the sound of this life of man on earth
his endless radio broadcasts and tv transmissions
newspapers rolling off endless rolls on rotary presses
the flow of his words and images
on endless typewriter ribbons and tapes
automatic writings and scrawlings
endless *poèmes dictés* by the unknown
Endless the calling on telephones to ends of earth
the waiting of lovers on station platforms
the crying of birds on hills and rooftops
the cawing and cawing of crows in the sky
the myriad churming of crickets
the running seas the crying waters
rising and falling on far shingles
the lapping of tides
in the Ides of autumn
salt kiss of creation
No end to the sea bells tolling
beyond the dams and dykes of life
and the calling and calling of bells
in empty churches and towers of time
No end to the calamitous enunciation
of hairy holy man
Endless the ever-unwinding
watchspring heart of the world
shimmering in time
shining through space
Endless the tourist-boats through it
bateaux mouches in endless canals

millions of windows aflame in sunset
the City burns with leftover light
the red light districts rock and glow
with endless porn and neon cocks
and vibrators vibrating endlessly
in lonely topfloor rooms of leaning houses
Endless the munching
on the meat-sandwiches of lust
the juicy steaks of love
endless dreams and orgasms
fertility rites and rites of passage
and flights of fertile birds over rooftops
and the dropping of eggs in nests and wombs
the tempts and attempts of the flesh
in furnished rooms of love
where sings the stricken dove
No end to the birthing of babies
where love or lust has lain
no end to the sweet birth of consciousness
no end to the bitter deaths of it in vain
No end no end to the withering
of fur and fruit and flesh so passing fair
and the neon mermaids
singing each to each somewhere
Endless the slight variations
of the utterly familiar
the fires of youth the embers of age
the rage of the poet born again
No end no end to any and all creation
in the mute dance of molecules
All is transmuted All is muted
and all cries out again again
Endless the waiting for God and Godot
the absurd actions absurd plans and plays
dilemmas and delays

Absurd and waiting without action
for the withering away of war
and the withering away of the state
Insane the waiting without action
for the insane ending!
Endless the wars of good and evil
the flips of fate the trips of hate
endless nukes and faults all failing-safe
in endless chain reactions of the final flash
while the White Bicycles of protest
still slowly circle round it
For there will be an end to the dogfaced gods
in wingtip shoes in Gucci slippers
in Texas boots and tin hats
in bunkers pressing buttons
For there is no end to the hopeful choices
still to be chosen
the dark minds lighted
the paths of glory
the green giants of chance
the fish-hooks of hope in the sloughs of despond
the hills in the distance the birds in the bush
hidden streams of light and unheard melodies
sessions of sweet silent thought
stately pleasure domes decreed
and the happy deaths of the heart every day
the cocks of clay
the feet in running shoes
upon the quai
And there is no end
to the doors of perception still to be opened
and the jet-streams of light
in the upper air of the spirit of man
in the outer space inside us
in the Amsterdams of yin & yang

Endless rubaiyats and endless beatitudes
endless shangri-las endless nirvanas
sutras and mantras
satoris and sensaras
Bodhiramas and Boddhisatvas
karmas and karmapas!
Endless singing Shivas dancing
on the smoking wombs of ecstasy!
Shining! Transcendent!
into the crystal night of time
in the endless silence of the soul
in the long loud tale of man
in his endless sound and fury
signifying everything
with his endless hallucinations
adorations annihilations illuminations
erections and exhibitions
fascismo and machismo
circuses of the soul astray
merrygorounds of the imagination
coney island of the mindless
endless poem dictated
by the uncollected voice
of the collective unconscious
blear upon the tracks of time!

In the last days of Alexandria
The day before Waterloo
The dancing continues
There is a sound of revelry by night

Amsterdam, July 1980

Index of Titles and First Lines

INDEX

A Meeting of Eyes in Mexico, 150
A Phoenix at Fifty, 105
A poet is born, 110
A Sweet Flying Dream, 182
Above Taos now, 107
Adieu À Charlot, 199
Alienation: Two Bees, 144
An Elegy on the Death of Kenneth Patchen, 110
An Elegy to Dispel Gloom, 197
An Imaginary Happening, London, 113
And I heard the learned astronomer, 146
And She 'Like a Young Year . . .', 12
And she 'like a young year . . .', 12
And the Arabs Asked Terrible Questions . . ., 5
And the Arabs asked terrible questions, 5
Assassination Raga, 81
At new age fifty, 105
At the stoplight waiting for the light, 184
Autobiography, 47
Away above a Harborful . . ., 3
Away above a harborful, 3

Baseball Canto, 125
By the great river Deschutes, 164

Caw Caw Caw, 179
Come Lie with Me and Be My Love, 72
Come lie with me and be my love, 72
Constantly Risking Absurdity . . ., 43

Constantly risking absurdity and death, 43

Deep Chess, 148
Director of Alienation, 133
Dog, 56
Dove sta amore . . ., 46
Dove sta amore, 46

Eight People on a Golf Course and One Bird of Freedom Flying over, 154
Endless Life, 210
Endless the splendid life of the world, 210

For All I Know Maybe She Was Happier, 9
For all I know maybe she was happier, 9
For years the old Italians have been dying, 175
Fortune . . ., 10
Fortune has its cookies to give out, 10

Heaven . . ., 17
Heaven was only half as far that night, 17
Hidden Door, 65
Hidden door dead secret, 65
Home Home Home, 189
Horses at Dawn, 167
Humankind can indeed bear, 103

I am leading a quiet life, 47
I Am Waiting, 59
I am waiting for my case to come up, 59

I came upon them in the cabin—, 144

I didn't get much sleep last night, 69

I had just ordered a fishplate at the counter when, 100

I Have Not Lain with Beauty All My Life . . . , 39

I have not lain with beauty all my life, 39

I laugh to hear me say what I am saying, 128

I put on the diving mask and went down, 168

I walked into a logo in the Teatro Melisso, 117

I was conceived in the summer of Nineteen Eighteen, 97

In a dream within a dream I dreamt a dream, 170

In a Time of Revolution For Instance, 100

In Golden Gate Park that Day . . . , 36

In Golden Gate Park that day, 36

In Goya's Greatest Scenes We Seem to See . . . , 27

In Goya's greatest scenes we seem to see, 27

In Hintertime Praxiteles . . . , 4

In Hintertime Praxiteles, 4

In the lower left-hand corner, 113

Into the Deeper Pools . . . , 168

It takes a fast car, 139

It Was a Face which Darkness Could Kill . . . , 13

It was a face which darkness could kill, 13

Knock knock on wooden Russia!, 119

Laughing and Crying, 127

Let us not sit upon the ground, 197

Life itself like championship chess, 148

Looking in the mirrors at Macy's, 133

Lost Parents, 139

Midnight Moscow Airport, 88

Modern Poetry Is Prose (But It is Saying Plenty), 208

Moscow in the Wilderness, Segovia in the Snow, 88

Night Light, 130

Night, night, 130

Night's black mirror is broken, 147

Not Like Dante . . . , 41

Not like Dante, 41

Olber's Paradox, 146

On the coast of Chile where Neruda lived, 152

On the green riverbank, 163

On the Transsiberian, 119

One grand boulevard with trees, 120

People Getting Divorced, 141

People getting divorced, 141

Poets, come out of your closets, 156

Populist Manifesto, 156

Pound at Spoleto, 117

Reading Apollinaire by the Rogue River, 165

Reading Apollinaire here, 165

Reading Yeats I Do Not Think . . . , 21

Reading Yeats I do not think of Ireland, 21

Recipe for Happiness in Khabarovsy or Anyplace, 120

Retired Ballerinas, Central Park West, 207

Retired ballerinas on winter afternoons, 207

Rough Song of Animals Dying, 170

Salute, 121

San Jose Symphony Reception, 193

Sarolla's Women in their Picture Hats . . . , 7

Sarolla's women in their Picture hats, 7

See It Was Like This When . . . , 38

See it was like this when, 38
Short Story on a Painting of Gustav Klimt, 142
Sometime During Eternity . . . , 31
Sometime during eternity some guys show up, 31
Sons of Whitman, sons of Poe, 199
Stone Reality Meditation, 103
Suddenly, 150
Sunrise, Bolinas, 104
Sweet and Various the Woodlark . . . , 23
Sweet and various the woodlark, 23

That Fellow on the Boattrain Who Insisted . . . , 16
That fellow on the boattrain who insisted, 16
The bald man in plaid playing the harpsichord, 193
The Billboard Painters, 184
'The curious upward stumbling motion . . .', 114
The dog trots freely in the street, 56
The General Song of Humanity, 152
The Great Chinese Dragon, 73
The great Chinese dragon which is the greatest dragon . . . , 73
The horses the horses the wild horses at dawn, 167
The Man Who Rode Away, 107
The Old Italians Dying, 175
The Old Sailors, 163
The Pennycandystore beyond the El . . . , 45
The pennycandystore beyond the El, 45
The phoenix flies higher & higher, 154
The Poet's Eye Obscenely Seeing . . . , 29
The poet's eye obscenely seeing, 29
The Sea and Ourselves at Cape Ann, 179

The two white-overalled white-capped, 184
The World Is a Beautiful Place . . . , 18
The world is a beautiful place, 18
There's a breathless hush on the freeway tonight, 137
They are kneeling upright on a flowered bed, 142
They Were Putting up the Statue . . . , 33
They were putting up the statue, 33
Third World Calling, 123
This little heart that remembers, 104
This loud morning, 123
Thoughts to a Concerto of Telemann, 114
To every animal who eats or shoots his own kind, 121
Toc Toc: A Couple Observed, 116
Today I'll write white on white, 194
True Confessional, 97
Tune in to a raga, 81
Two Scavengers in a Truck, Two Beautiful People in a Mercedes, 184

Underwear, 69
Upon Reflection, 147

Watching baseball, 124
We were two naked, 182
What Could She Say to the Fantastic Foolybear . . . , 35
What could she say to the fantastic foolybear, 35
Where are they going, 189
White on White, 194
Wild Dreams of a New Beginning, 137
Wild Life Cameo, Early Morn, 164
With Bells for Hooves in Sounding Streets . . . , 14
With bells for hooves in sounding streets, 14
Without closing its wings, 116

Some New Directions Paperbooks

Walter Abish, *Alphabetical Africa*. NDP375.
 In the Future Perfect. NDP440.
 Minds Meet. NDP387.
Illangô Adigal, *Shilappadikaram*. NDP162.
Alain, *The Gods*. NDP382
Wayne Andrews. *Voltaire*. NDP519.
David Antin, *Talking at the Boundaries*. NDP388.
G. Apollinaire, *Selected Writings*.† NDP310.
Djuna Barnes, *Nightwood*. NDP98.
Charles Baudelaire, *Flowers of Evil*.† NDP71,
 Paris Spleen. NDP294.
Martin Bax, *The Hospital Ship*. NDP402.
Gottfried Benn, *Primal Vision*.† NDP322.
Wolfgang Borchert, *The Man Outside*. NDP319.
Jorge Luis Borges, *Labyrinths*. NDP186.
Jean-Francois Bory, *Once Again* NDP256.
E. Brock, *Here. Now. Always*. NDP429.
 The Portraits & The Poses. NDP360.
 The River and the Train. NDP478.
Buddha, *The Dhammapada*. NDP188.
Frederick Busch, *Domestic Particulars*. NDP413.
 Manual Labor. NDP376.
Ernesto Cardenal, *Apocalypse*. NDP441. *In Cuba*.
 NDP377. *Zero Hour*. NDP502.
Hayden Carruth, *For You*. NDP298.
 From Snow and Rock, from Chaos. NDP349.
Louis-Ferdinand Céline,
 Death on the Installment Plan NDP330.
 Journey to the End of the Night. NDP84.
Jean Cocteau, *The Holy Terrors*. NDP212.
 The Infernal Machine. NDP235.
M. Cohen, *Monday Rhetoric*. NDP352.
Robert Coles, *Irony in the Mind's Life*. NDP459.
Cid Corman, *Livingdying*. NDP289.
 Sun Rock Man. NDP318.
Gregory Corso, *Elegiac Feelings*. NDP299.
 Happy Birthday of Death. NDP86.
 Long Live Man. NDP127.
Robert Creeley, *Hello*. NDP451.
 Later. NDP488.
Edward Dahlberg, *Reader*. NDP246.
 Because I Was Flesh. NDP227.
Osamu Dazai, *The Setting Sun*. NDP258.
 No Longer Human. NDP357.
Coleman Dowell, *Mrs. October . . .* NDP368.
 Too Much Flesh and Jabez. NDP447.
Robert Duncan, *Bending the Bow*. NDP255.
 The Opening of the Field. NDP356.
 Roots and Branches. NDP275.
Dutch "Fiftiers," *Living Space*. NDP493.
Richard Eberhart, *Selected Poems*. NDP198.
E. F. Edinger, *Melville's Moby-Dick*. NDP460.
Russell Edson, *The Falling Sickness*. NDP389.
Wm. Empson, *7 Types of Ambiguity*. NDP204.
 Some Versions of Pastoral. NDP92.
Wm. Everson, *Man-Fate*, NDP369.
 The Residual Years. NDP263.
Lawrence Ferlinghetti, *Her*. NDP88.
 A Coney Island of the Mind. NDP74.
 Endless Life. NDP516.
 The Mexican Night. NDP300.
 The Secret Meaning of Things. NDP268.
 Starting from San Francisco. NDP220.
 Tyrannus Nix?. NDP288.
 Unfair Arguments . . . NDP143
 Who Are We Now? NDP425.
Ronald Firbank. *Five Novels*. NDP518.
F. Scott Fitzgerald, *The Crack-up*. NDP54.
Robert Fitzgerald, *Spring Shade*. NDP311.
Gustave Flaubert, *Dictionary*. NDP230.
Gandhi, *Gandhi on Non-Violence*. NDP197.
Goethe, *Faust*, Part I. NDP70.
Henry Green. *Back*. NDP517.
Allen Grossman, *The Woman on the Bridge*
 Over the Chicago River. NDP473.
John Hawkes, *The Beetle Leg*. NDP239.
 The Blood Oranges. NDP338.
 The Cannibal. NDP123.
 Death Sleep & The Traveler. NDP393.
 The Innocent Party. NDP238.
 The Lime Twig. NDP95.
 The Owl. NDP443.
Second Skin. NDP146.
 Travesty. NDP430.
A. Hayes, *A Wreath of Christmas Poems*.
 NDP347.
Samuel Hazo. *To Paris*. NDP512.
H. D., *End to Torment*. NDP476.
 Helen in Egypt. NDP380.
 Hermetic Definition. NDP343.
 Trilogy. NDP362.
Robert E. Helbling, *Heinrich von Kleist,* NDP390.
Hermann Hesse, *Siddhartha*. NDP65.
C. Isherwood, *All the Conspirators*. NDP480.
 The Berlin Stories. NDP134.
Philippe Jaccottet, *Seedtime*. NDP428.
Alfred Jarry, *The Supermale*. NDP426.
 Ubu Roi. NDP105.
Robinson Jeffers, *Cawdor and Media*. NDP293.
James Joyce, *Stephen Hero*. NDP133.
 James Joyce/Finnegans Wake. NDP331.
Franz Kafka, *Amerika*. NDP117.
Bob Kaufman,
 The Ancient Rain. NDP514.
 Solitudes Crowded with Loneliness. NDP199.
Hugh Kenner, *Wyndham Lewis*. NDP167.
Kenyon Critics, *G. M. Hopkins*. NDP355.
H. von Kleist, *Prince Friedrich of Homburg*.
 NDP462.
Elaine Kraf, *The Princess of 72nd St*. NDP494.
P. Lal, *Great Sanskrit Plays*. NDP142.
Lautréamont, *Maldoror*. NDP207.
Irving Layton, *Selected Poems*. NDP431.
Denise Levertov, *Collected Earlier*. NDP475.
 Footprints. NDP344.
 The Freeing of the Dust. NDP401.
 The Jacob's Ladder. NDP112.
 Life in the Forest. NDP461.
 The Poet in the World. NDP363.
 Relearning the Alphabet. NDP290.
 The Sorrow Dance. NDP222.
 To Stay Alive. NDP325.
Harry Levin, *James Joyce*. NDP87.
Li Ch'ing-chao, *Complete Poems*. NDP492.
Enrique Lihn, *The Dark Room*.† NDP452.
García Lorca, *The Cricket Sings*.† NDP506.
 Deep Song. NDP503.
 Five Plays. NDP232.
 Selected Poems.† NDP114.
 Three Tragedies. NDP52.
Michael McClure, *Gorf*. NDP416.
 Antechamber. NDP455.
 Jaguar Skies. NDP400.
 Josephine: The Mouse Singer. NDP496.
Carson McCullers, *The Member of the*
 Wedding. (Playscript) NDP153.
Thomas Merton, *Asian Journal*. NDP394.
 Collected Poems. NDP504.
 Gandhi on Non-Violence. NDP197.
 News Seeds of Contemplation. NDP337.
 Raids on the Unspeakable. NDP213.
 Selected Poems. NDP85.
 The Way of Chuang Tzu. NDP276.
 The Wisdom of the Desert. NDP295.
 Zen and the Birds of Appetite. NDP261.
Henry Miller, *The Air-Conditioned Nightmare*.
 NDP302.
 Big Sur & The Oranges. NDP161.
 The Books in My Life. NDP280.
 The Colossus of Maroussi. NDP75.
 The Cosmological Eye. NDP109.
 Henry Miller on Writing. NDP151.
 The Henry Miller Reader. NDP269.
 Just Wild About Harry. NDP479.
 The Smile at the Foot of the Ladder. NDP386.
 Stand Still-Like the Hummingbird. NDP236.
 The Time of the Assassins. NDP115.
Y. Mishima, *Confessions of a Mask*. NDP253.
 Death in Midsummer. NDP215.
Eugenio Montale, *It Depends*.† NDP507.
 New Poems. NDP410.
 Selected Poems.† NDP193.
Vladimir Nabokov, *Nikolai Gogol*. NDP78.
 Laughter in the Dark. NDP470.
 The Real Life of Sebastian Knight. NDP432.
P. Neruda, *The Captain's Verses*.† NDP345.
 Residence on Earth.† NDP340.

New Directions in Prose & Poetry (Anthology).
  Available from #17 forward. #42, Fall 1981.
Robert Nichols, Arrival. NDP437.
  Exile. NDP485. Garh City. NDP450.
  Harditts in Sawna. NDP470.
Charles Olson. Selected Writings. NDP231.
Toby Olson, The Life of Jesus. NDP417.
George Oppen, Collected Poems. NDP418.
Wilfred Owen, Collected Peoms. NDP210.
Nicanor Parra, Emergency Poems.† NDP333.
  Poems and Antipoems.† NDP242.
Boris Pasternak, Safe Conduct. NDP77.
Kenneth Patchen. Aflame and Afun. NDP292.
  Because It Is. NDP83.
  But Even So. NDP265.
  Collected Poems. NDP284.
  Doubleheader. NDP211.
  Hallelujah Anyway. NDP219.
  In Quest of Candlelighters. NDP334.
  Memoirs of a Shy Pornographer. NDP205.
  Selected Poems. NDP160.
Octavio Paz, Configurations.† NDP303.
  A Draft of Shadows.† NDP489.
  Eagle or Sun?† NDP422.
  Early Poems.† NDP354.
Plays for a New Theater. (Anth.) NDP216.
J. A. Porter, Eelgrass. NDP438.
Ezra Pound, ABC of Reading. NDP89.
  Classic Noh Theatre of Japan. NDP79.
  Confucius. NDP285.
  Confucius to Cummings. (Anth.) NDP126.
  Gaudier Brzeska. NDP372.
  Guide to Kulchur. NDP257.
  Literary Essays. NDP250.
  Love Poems of Ancient Egypt. NDP178.
  Pound/Joyce. NDP296.
  Selected Cantos. NDP304.
  Selected Letters 1907-1941. NDP317.
  Selected Poems. NDP66.
  The Spirit of Romance. NDP266.
  Translations.† (Enlarged Edition) NDP145.
James Purdy, Children Is All. NDP327.
Raymond Queneau, The Bark Tree. NDP314.
  Exercises in Style. NDP513.
  The Sunday of Life. NDP433.
  We Always Treat Women Too Well. NDP515.
Mary de Rachewiltz, Ezra Pound. NDP405.
M. Randall, Part of the Solution. NDP350.
John Crowe Ransom, Beating the Bushes.
  NDP324.
Raja Rao, Kanthapura. NDP224.
Herbert Read, The Green Child. NDP208.
P. Reverdy, Selected Poems.† NDP346.
Kenneth Rexroth, Collected Longer Poems.
  NDP309.
  Collected Shorter Poems. NDP243.
  The Morning Star. NDP490.
  New Poems. NDP383.
  100 More Poems from the Chinese. NDP308.
  100 More Poems from the Japanese. NDP420.
  100 Poems from the Chinese. NDP192.
  100 Poems from the Japanese.† NDP147.
Rainer Maria Rilke, Poems from
  The Book of Hours. NDP408.
  Possibility of Being. (Poems). NDP436.
  Where Silence Reigns. (Prose). NDP464.
Arthur Rimbaud, Illuminations.† NDP56.
  Season in Hell & Drunken Boat.† NDP97.
Edouard Roditi, Delights of Turkey. NDP445.
Selden Rodman, Tongues of Fallen Angels.
  NDP373.
Jerome Rothenberg, Poland/1931. NDP379.
  Pre-Faces. NDP511.
  Seneca Journal. NDP448.
  Vienna Blood. NDP498.
Saigyo,† Mirror for the Moon. NDP465.
Saikaku Ihara. The Life of an Amorous
  Woman. NDP270.
St. John of the Cross, Poems.† NDP341.
Jean-Paul Sartre, Baudelaire. NDP233.

Nausea. NDP82.
  The Wall (Intimacy). NDP272.
Delmore Schwartz, Selected Poems. NDP241.
  In Dreams Begin Responsibilities. NDP454.
Kazuko Shiraishi, Seaons of Sacred Lust.
  NDP453.
Stevie Smith, Selected Poems, NDP159.
Gary Snyder, The Back Country. NDP249.
  Earth House Hold. NDP267.
  Myths and Texts. NDP457.
  The Real Work. NDP499.
  Regarding Wave. NDP306.
  Turtle Island. NDP381.
Enid Starkie, Rimbaud. NDP254.
Robert Steiner, Bathers. NDP495.
Stendhal, The Telegraph. NDP108.
Jules Supervielle, Selected Writings.† NDP209.
W. Sutton, American Free Verse. NDP351.
Nathaniel Tarn, Lyrics . . . Bride of God. NDP391.
Dylan Thomas, Adventures in the Skin Trade.
  NDP183.
  A Child's Christmas in Wales. NDP181.
  Collected Poems 1934-1952. NDP316.
  The Doctor and the Devils. NDP297.
  Portrait of the Artist as a Young Dog.
  NDP51.
  Quite Early One Morning. NDP90.
  Under Milk Wood. NDP73.
Lionel Trilling. E. M. Forster. NDP189.
Martin Turnell. Art of French Fiction. NDP251.
  Baudelaire. NDP336.
  Rise of the French Novel. NDP474.
Paul Valéry, Selected Writings.† NDP184.
P. Van Ostaijen, Feasts of Fear & Agony.
  NDP411.
Elio Vittorini, A Vittorini Omnibus. NDP366.
  Women of Messina. NDP365.
Vernon Watkins, Selected Poems. NDP221.
Nathanael West, Miss Lonelyhearts &
  Day of the Locust. NDP125.
J. Williams, An Ear in Bartram's Tree. NDP335.
Tennessee Williams, Camino Real, NDP301.
  Cat on a Hot Tin Roof. NDP398.
  Dragon Country. NDP287.
  The Glass Menagerie. NDP218.
  Hard Candy. NDP225.
  In the Winter of Cities. NDP154.
  A Lovely Sunday for Creve Coeur. NDP497.
  One Arm & Other Stories. NDP237.
  A Streetcar Named Desire. NDP501.
  Sweet Bird of Youth. NDP409.
  Twenty-Seven Wagons Full of Cotton. NDP217.
  Two-Character Play. NDP483.
  Vieux Carré. NDP482.
  Where I Live. NDP468.
William Carlos Williams.
  The Autobiography. NDP223.
  The Build-up. NDP223.
  The Farmers' Daughters. NDP106.
  I Wanted to Write a Poem. NDP469.
  Imaginations. NDP329.
  In the American Grain. NDP53.
  In the Money. NDP240.
  Many Loves. NDP191.
  Paterson. Complete. NDP152.
  Pictures form Brueghel. NDP118.
  The Selected Essays. NDP273.
  Selected Poems. NDP131.
  A Voyage to Pagany. NDP307.
  White Mule. NDP226.
  W. C. Williams Reader. NDP282.
Yvor Winters, E. A. Robinson. NDP326.
Wisdom Books: Ancient Egyptians, NDP467.
  Early Buddhists, NDP444; English Mystics,
  NDP466; Forest (Hindu), NDP414; Jewish
  Mystics, NDP423; Spanish Mystics, NDP442;
  St. Francis, NDP477; Sufi, NDP424; Taoists,
  NDP509; Wisdom of the Desert, NDP295; Zen
  Masters, NDP415.

For complete listing request complete catalog from
New Directions, 80 Eighth Avenue, New York 10011

† Bilingual